Praise for

STEFANIE WILDER-TAYLOR

and her collections of humorous
essays on parenting and life

– – – – – – – – – – – –

"More fun than an all-little-person nativity scene."

—Chelsea Handler

"Twisted and wrong and absolutely hysterical."

—Jen Lancaster

"This book is hilarious. It's so real and funny. . . . I love it!"

—Molly Shannon

"Funny. . . . If you want to get inside a new mom's neurosis . . .
this book is for you."

—*Chicago Tribune*

"Her sharp wit takes center stage."

—*BookPage*

"Hilarious from cover to cover. Wilder-Taylor has a knack
for both winding up in good stories and telling them."

—MamaPop.com

"Every new mom has to learn these things, so why not enjoy
some laughs along the way?"

—*Hartford Courant*

"You can't help but love her. The world would be a better
place if she were the head Mommy."

—*Mississippi Press*

GUMMI BEARS
SHOULD
NOT BE
ORGANIC

And Other Opinions
I Can't Back Up with Facts

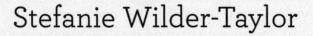

Stefanie Wilder-Taylor

GALLERY BOOKS

New York London Toronto Sydney New Delhi

G

GALLERY BOOKS
An Imprint of Simon & Schuster, Inc.
1230 Avenue of the Americas
New York, NY 10020

First Gallery Books trade paperback edition April 2015

GALLERY BOOKS and colophon are registered trademarks of Simon & Schuster, Inc.

For information about special discounts for bulk purchases, please contact Simon & Schuster Special Sales at 1-866-506-1949 or business@simonandschuster.com.

The Simon & Schuster Speakers Bureau can bring authors to your live event. For more information or to book an event contact the Simon & Schuster Speakers Bureau at 1-866-248-3049 or visit our website at www.simonspeakers.com.

Interior design by Jaime Putorti

Manufactured in the United States of America

10 9 8 7 6 5 4 3 2 1

Library of Congress Cataloging-in-Publication Data is available.

ISBN 978-1-4767-8730-5
ISBN 978-1-4767-8731-2 (ebook)

For my family—Jon, Elby, Sadie and Matilda—

without you there would be no book to write.

Acknowledgments

I have so many people to acknowledge and so little time due to *so many children* and so little childcare, but here goes: Thank you to Jennifer Bergstrom (the big Cha Cha at S&S) who believes in me time after time. I will always be grateful that you started my career! To Lauren McKenna, my super-fab editor for hearing my voice, listening to my neuroses (yes plural), having incredible vision, and adding sharp jokes! Elana Cohen, thank you for your great insights and always being on the other end of the phone in a crisis! Jennifer Robinson (J-Rob), can't wait to work on this with you again! And, of course, my agent, Alan Nevins, thank you for your guidance, wisdom, and really getting my humor!

Thank you to my Mom Friends: Lara Tochner, Julie Kasem, Cecily Lerner, and Kelly Hunter for keeping it real, helping me stay sane, listening to my ideas, giving me support, being my foundation, and making me laugh. You guys all set great examples in parenting! Thanks to Deirdre Walsh for very quickly going from my school mom friend to my Person! You've saved my ass on more than one occasion!

Wendi Aarons, girl, I owe you big-time for your super-swift, laugh-out-loud, in-the-nick-of-time help! They were, in fact, all gems.

Shout-out to my brother, Michael Wilder, and my SIL Racquel, and their brood! I couldn't ask for a more supportive family to muddle through all this with me!

Lisa Sundstedt, heeeeelllloooo! Your friendship and support for over twenty years means everything.

Thank you so much to Bronwen O'Keefe and Kim Powers for giving my voice and humor such an incredible home at NickMom. I'm forever in your debt. And to Hugh Fink: I'm so glad I had the incredible fortune to partner up with you! You make everything better!

Also, to Lori Nasso, Anna Lotto, Anna Lefler, Katie Massa Kennedy, Danielle Koenig, Beth Armogida, thanks for making me sound way smarter than I am!

A special thanks to all my Facebook friends who took the time to answer my queries, add your opinions, and keep my spirits up! I am so grateful!

Acknowledgments

To my thoughtful, sweet, smart, beautiful kids. Elby, Sadie, and Matilda: I am crazy, crazy, crazy for you. I hope I'm doing okay in the mom department. You are killing it in the kid department.

And, last but not least, my husband, Jon: Thank you for reading every chapter, giving me hilarious jokes, putting up with my insanity, bringing me home CCC, and letting me drive. I still sometimes can't believe how much I lucked out. I love you.

Contents

Contents

GUMMI BEARS

SHOULD

NOT BE

ORGANIC

Introduction

The main complaint I have about parenting (and if you've read my other books you'll know my list of complaints is long) is that there is no one perfect way to do it. Although there are plenty of people who claim otherwise. There are more experts, books, and parenting philosophies than you can shake a positive EPT stick at, and a lot of them have differing views. Should I force my kids to play the violin until their fingers bleed while yelling at them in Mandarin and Cantonese, à la the Tiger Mom? Or, as per the French, should I be raising my kids on three buttered croissants a day while smoking, drinking red wine, and having a ménage à trois? Obviously I'm kidding; croissants are super fattening.

It's difficult enough to digest all the information, let alone to distill it into practice. Especially in that first year.

That first year is a beeyotch. That first year I felt like I'd been dropped on a desert island with a naked stranger who was constantly hungry and crying for no discernible reason. It was sort of like being a contestant on *Survivor*, except add in bleeding nipples and instead of a million-dollar prize substitute a drained bank account. But hold on, I'm making it sound better than it is.

I read way too much about parenting that first year because I had important decisions to make: If I don't breast-feed, will my baby's future be limited to folding T-shirts at Old Navy for a living? If I let her cry it out, will she not be able to make attachments and grow up to be a sociopath? Okay, I may have been a little paranoid. But with good reason. When I wanted to stop breast-feeding I made the mistake of Googling it and came across this from BabyCenter: "One large study by the National Institute of Environmental Health Sciences showed that children who are breastfed have a twenty percent lower risk of dying between the ages of 28 days and one year than children who weren't breastfed." *What?* Yeah. Have fun weaning!

And my new-mom friends weren't of any help, because when I told them I was thinking of quitting breast-feeding they were like, "Did you read that study on BabyCenter? No? Let me e-mail it to you!"

As my daughter got older, I'm ashamed to say I became even more neurotic, because I realized I had a child. My baby was no longer just a little lump of clay, incapable of storing memories for her future tell-all memoirs. The free ride through Amnesia Town had just screeched to a stop in Every-Decision-Has-a-Consequence-Ville. I mean, I spent so much time researching preschools you'd think my kid was getting an experimental medical procedure and not just learning the proper way to hold a crayon.

But then, a few years later, something miraculous happened: I had twins. Twin girls. And I had them six weeks early (clearly that part sucked, but hang on). When your kids' health is in crisis, it has a way of putting things in perspective. Suddenly I had no time to worry about stupid stuff, such as whether I should make sure they tried strained peas before we moved on to pears so that they wouldn't get hooked on the sweet sweet taste of fruit and never want to try a vegetable. Honestly, I could give a fuck. I was far too busy trying to keep them alive while maintaining a stranglehold on my sanity. The twins had colic, one of them wasn't eating, and I hadn't showered since my third trimester.

And through that experience, in my strive for balance and serenity, a glorious new parenting style emerged. Actually it's more of a parenting nonstyle—a "whatever works" approach. It's a perfect cocktail made from a blend of one part neurosis and two parts "this is my eighth kid."

I used disposable diapers and never touched a bottle sterilizer, but I buy organic chicken at Whole Foods because I don't want my daughters getting their periods at eight. I also buy Goldfish crackers in bulk and I allow my kids plenty of TV, but I keep a very regular bedtime routine. I don't insist on a bath every night (and sometimes teeth brushing gets pushed off until morning), but story time is sacred. Maybe that's my parenting philosophy: read! But I'm not going to have that embroidered onto a pillow anytime soon.

I care about things like how many cookies they eat or how much TV they watch, but I temper that with being aware of how those factors are actually affecting them and do not just base it on the latest scare study. They may love TV, but it doesn't seem to be giving them ADD or making them lose interest in using their imaginations. So, do they sometimes watch a shitload of it in one day? Yeah. And guess what—sometimes they don't watch TV at all! You don't know what I'm going to do next! I'm a crazy renegade!

I'm not the sweets police either; when my kids have had a couple of cookies for dessert and they ask if they can have one more, I give it to them! Some may think I'm giving childhood obesity the finger, but I'm just crazy like that.

I don't discipline my children just for the sake of having a "stance on discipline." I let my kids' personalities dictate which tactic to use. My oldest daughter rarely ever needs a time-out or for me to raise my voice. She's eager to please, sensitive, and easy to redirect. Yet one of my twins has been known to have five time-outs in one day. It works for her.

So guess what: this parenting nonstyle is working for me. And it can work for you, too! I don't believe for a minute that tiger moms are superior mothers, or that working moms suck, or that stay-at-home moms are more blessed, or that there is any magic answer to any of our age-old parenting problems—except maybe sleep, and that magic answer is Benadryl. (I'm joking! Don't start writing me nasty e-mails yet; this is only the introduction, you need to pace yourself.)

I say we have to take back our power! Grow some mama cojones and fight the man! Who is the man? I don't know, exactly, but he's very busy writing studies aimed at scaring the shit out of us and making us feel like we suck ass at parenting.

So let me bottom-line my position on this: I absolutely love my kids and love parenting them. I also know I'm far from perfect. But after spending enough time freaking out over everything, I've learned what studies, schools of thought, and parenting trends are worth my attention and what to just tune out.

And in case you're wondering, that Tiger Mom thing? Never read it.

Overparenting:
Are We Raising Entitled,
Dependent, Neurotic Kids?
Or Are We Just Attentive?

My name is Stefanie and I'm an overparent. Admitting it is the first step, right? Up until recently I was smugly standing in judgment of other overparents—you know, the ones who are crazily overprotective, handicapping their kids' development by doing everything for them for fear of their ever having a skinned knee or a hurt feeling, leaving them sheltered and neurotic and living in their parents' guesthouse at thirty? Yeah, those parents. I wasn't like them at all.

Then one day, my almost-ten-year-old asked me for a bagel, and like Pavlov's dog I jumped up from my desk, ran to the toaster oven, popped a bagel in, and then sat back down to work. When the toaster dinged, she came to get me. "Mom. My bagel's done."

"Oh, okay," I said, jumping back up to finish the bagel-making process despite being right in the middle of something. But suddenly, a genius plan formulated in my brain—a plan that would enable me to *not have to get up*—a plan that I could hardly believe I hadn't thought of sooner. I decided to put that plan right into action. "Honey, why don't you just go ahead and put the cream cheese on it yourself?" I suggested. And then I waited.

"Okay," she said. *Sweet Jesus, I'm so golden!* I thought. *This is the start of a new era! Think of all the work I can get done while my child is off doing stuff for herself! Of course she should be doing her own bagel prep. It's about time!* I mentally patted myself on the back for teaching my child independence and helping bring out her inner resourcefulness. This would be a real turning point! Future bagel-making opportunities would be endless. I mean, hell, we're Jews.

Four minutes later my kid came back to me.

"Mom, I put the bagel on the plate but I'm not that good at spreading cream cheese. Can you please do it?" It was at that moment that I realized things were way worse than I thought. My kid was completely helpless, and it was my own fault. My daughter wasn't lazy; it's just that by always spreading her cream cheese—either to be helpful or out of my own form of laziness (it was just easier to do it myself),

I'd robbed her of confidence in her cream-cheese-spreading abilities.

When I was a kid I could spread cream cheese on a bagel like a motherfucker. Not only that, but by the time I was six I was buttering up bread and popping it into the toaster all on my own, letting the sparks fly where they might and then pulling it out with a fork. I didn't even know that having someone else do it for me was an option—mainly because *it wasn't*. If I wanted bread I had to climb up on the counter, using drawer handles as toeholds, and pull it down myself. My kids wouldn't dream of doing something as strenuous as climbing up on the countertop. We have step stools. In fact, there is so little physical exertion going on in my house it's like I'm raising veal.

It was a little shocking when I realized that I am part of the overparenting problem, but I can see why I was in denial. It was too easy to compare myself to parents around me and feel like I'm way ahead of the game!

I'm definitely not as bad as one mom I know who texted me while I was driving her eight-year-old daughter to an activity with my daughter. The message said: "If you stop for a snack, please make sure Penelope washes her hands first!" Really? It felt wrong on so many levels. I mean, first of all, I don't believe that kids should be washing their hands all the time. How are their bodies going to learn to fight off germs on their own if we're crippling their immune systems by doing all the heavy lifting? Stop rinsing off all the bacteria and let the immune system do its job! But second, if you're going to let your kid go off with someone else, you've got to *let them go* and assume it won't be a smoking, drinking, no-booster-seat-using free-for-all. I mean, you're leaving them with another parent, not Lindsay Lohan.

That wasn't an isolated incident either. I've run into lots of situations that made me feel "not that bad" in comparison. We've all seen the parents who roll their kids around in a stroller until they're practically tweens. I don't get that. You ever see a giant kid in a stroller who can brake Fred Flintstone–style because their feet are dragging on the ground? What's their plan? Are they going to keep the kid in there until they can transfer them to a Rascal scooter when they're seventy? And these are the same parents who chase their kids around with snacks every fourteen seconds even though the kids aren't hungry—I guess it's tough to work up an appetite when you're pushed around in a stroller all day. Then there are the parents who can't part with the sippy cup. I once attempted to serve a seven-year-old some lemonade in a glass and the mom reacted like I'd just handed her kid a hunting rifle before she'd had the requisite safety training. "Oooh, I don't think she's ready to drink out of a glass yet."

So yeah, although I wasn't as bad as some, after Bagelgate I knew I needed to make some changes. If you, like me, are attempting to give your kids a little more freedom and expecting a higher level of functioning, be warned: not everyone will be on board.

One of the roadblocks you might meet if you're on this trek is the Parenting Police. These are the people who are "only trying to be helpful" by pointing out when you are being a neglectful parent. At best, these types of people can shame you into keeping a better eye on your kids or happily point out a possible consequence for your reckless behavior; at worst, they can call the cops on your ass.

One of my first acts of Operation Independence was allowing my kids to wander around a big room at the Museum of Natural History. There was one entrance to the large space and I positioned myself near it, but I let all three kids wander from animal to animal reading about each one's natural habitat and its predators *all by themselves*! Educational on so many levels! It wasn't super daring since I could eyeball all three of them the entire time, but I still felt confident it was a step in the right direction. Appar-

ently some other people didn't agree. Less than five minutes in, an alarmed-looking mother approached me with a
baby strapped to her chest, a toddler on a cute little fuzzy
monkey leash, and her free hand on the shoulder of one
of my twins. "Is this your daughter?" she asked, in a way
that would imply she'd just managed to botch a kidnapping
attempt.

"Um, yes," I said.

"She was just wandering around and she started talking to me! I asked her where her mom was and she said
she didn't know! So we walked around until she saw you!" I
didn't quite know what to say to that, so I just thanked her
a little too profusely. And then she added, "You can't be too
careful." Of course I immediately felt like a bad mommy.

But then I thought, *Isn't it enough that I took my kids to
the museum? Can't I count that as a parenting win for the day?*
Plus, she was in one contained space. It's not like I let her
loose at the dog track and told her to meet me back at the
door at six.

Even though I felt defensive, at least that mom was just
trying to be helpful. I was kind of lucky. These days there
are actual cases where well-meaning parents have been
reported and even arrested for things like allowing their
kids to spend a few hours at a park alone or play outside on

a scooter. In one case, a mom got arrested for simply letting her seven-year-old walk to a park that was a few blocks away by himself, mainly because the neighbors complained that known child molesters lived in the neighborhood. Although this happened in Florida, so . . . yeah. But when you read stuff like that it makes you realize what a giant cultural hurdle we have to jump in order to allow our kids to develop some autonomy, experience failure, and make mistakes.

Unfortunately, it's not just other parents who want to squelch our impulse to give the kids more freedom. My kids don't seem all that psyched by my change in attitude either. The other day I suggested my nine-year-old walk about five blocks through my quiet neighborhood to get to the house of a friend. She wouldn't have to cross any busy streets, and I could practically see her the whole way. She looked at me like I had suggested she juggle knives. "You want me to just walk alone?"

"Yes. I do!" I said. "I think I'm ready."

Of course, being ready doesn't mean I don't struggle. Once at a big crowded Los Angeles park, I left one of my twins playing on a seesaw while I took the other twin a few yards off to the bathroom. I tried to get the first one to come with us but she was happily playing, so I looked around, saw a ton of other kids and parents, and decided she'd be fine hanging out for five minutes. A few minutes later I walked back and scanned the sand for her red Angry Birds T-shirt, but I couldn't spot her in the sea of kids. I thought about how I told her I'd be right back and then started to fully panic and wondered if someone could've overheard me tell her to stay put and thought that would be a great opportunity to steal her. I suddenly remembered that John Walsh's son was *only five* when he was taken from a department store thirty years ago. It was at that moment that I really missed Xanax. Then, of course, I spotted her happy as a clam playing right where I'd left her and I realized, quite clearly, that I really really need to cut down on my *Dateline* intake.

It's hard not to be paranoid in our age of information and the Internet. I was talking to a friend of mine who's actually on the saner side about this and she agreed, saying, "Every time I get the guts to let my kids do something a bit more daring like, oh, swim at the pool without me being in with them, I come across some crazy story on Facebook about dry drowning—this phenomenon where kids breathe in water and then die of drowning later in the day seemingly with no symptoms!" Um, yeah! Read it! Googled it! Freaked out over it! Another friend said, "I have to take twenty minutes deciding if I should put toxic sunscreen on my kids or let them be exposed to dangerous sun rays because Huffington Post linked to two different articles about each subject this week." I'd read that too and became so paralyzed I almost didn't send my kids to camp that day. Almost. I'm neurotic, not insane.

All of this attention to overparenting has given birth to an equally annoying phenomenon: the people who go the complete other way with it—the ones who glorify parenting in the seventies as the *best time ever*! It seems like every day I see some blog post or another about how much better the seventies were because *we all just ran around unsupervised and used our imaginations! We didn't have electronics! None! We made up games! We played kick the can! Our parents just told us to go play and not to come back until the streetlights were on!* I'm sorry, but this sentiment is starting to get played out. I lived through that time and it wasn't all that fucking groovy. It was the underparenting of the seventies that has led to a lot of the overparenting a generation later!

I was a latchkey kid who walked home every day with a key around my neck on a piece of yarn. I had to let myself into an empty duplex after school, make a snack, and do my homework. It was lonely. Trust me, my mood ring was black *all the time*. And sure, we went out to play in vacant lots and random people's backyards with just the reminder "Don't forget your poncho, and stay away from panel vans!" But it wasn't safe! Shit sometimes went sideways and the adults in our lives were too busy watching *All My Children* and trying to heal their inner child to help us out. Growing up in the seventies is why Paxil is so popular now!

Some people are taking this whole concept really far. There's an adventure playground in Wales where they are trying to re-create the vacant-lot feel of playgrounds from decades ago. They supply the kids with old broken-down chairs, and a fire pit with cardboard and wood so kids can actually light stuff on fire. There's a creek and tire swing to get across it so kids can play just like they did in the good old 1970s. Apparently there are a few playground workers but parents are not welcome.

I'm not saying this is a horrible idea, but it's not exactly real life. If they really want to make it authentic, they should add a few bullies to terrorize the younger kids, helping to create lifelong generalized anxiety disorders, and a few "weird older brothers" to hang around providing what will only be described as "inappropriate touching" years later in therapy. I'm sorry, but shit like this makes me appreciate kids' staying in and playing Minecraft.

I guess the bottom line is I realize that I'm a little overprotective of my kids. I own it, and yet I'm trying to work on it. I know that kids are going to get lost. They will get scared. They will get sad and angry and fail. They're supposed to. It's our job to get out of their way and let them live a little. That's how kids develop grit, which is the most accurate predictor for who will do well in life. So I'm working on stepping aside. When my kids fight, I try to let them work it out on their own (unless I see blood). I refuse to schedule every moment of their day, which forces them to go outside and find stuff to do (provided I can still see them), and if they want a snack I tell them to just go get one! But every once in a while I still spread some cream cheese on my daughter's bagel. I'm only human. And plus, like I said, I'm motherfucking good at it!

I Don't Care About
Your Natural Childbirth

When my sister-in-law had her first baby she had four hours of labor, pushing briefly while holding her husband's hand and listening to her custom playlist of soothing New Age birthing tones. After just ten minutes, her beautiful baby boy slid out of her like a tiny effing miracle. Everything was perfect.

I've had two C-sections.

When I visited my sister-in-law in the hospital, she was gushing. She said things like, "It was the most natural experience of my entire life," and "It's like, now I understand what our bodies are made for. It all makes perfect sense!" She actually got teary at that realization. To be fair, this was totally out of character for her. She's from New Jersey. I'm guessing she was flying a little high from the drugs, but it still made me feel like I was missing out, like maybe my vagina hadn't been given a fair shot.

It's not that I wouldn't have been totally open to attempting to squeeze the baby out through my hoo-ha, but before I'd ever even gotten knocked up the first time, I'd been treated repeatedly for uterine fibroids, and after the last surgery my doctor announced, "I need to let you know that you won't be able to give birth vaginally." At the time, this hadn't exactly felt like a crushing blow. Wait, you mean I'll avoid painful labor and then the possibility of spending the next thirty years having to pee more frequently than a frat boy losing at beer pong? Say it isn't so! Yeah, it's safe to say I wasn't overly concerned.

Apparently, I was the only one who wasn't. I quickly discovered that a lot of women love nothing more than to compare stories about their labor. "What's your birth plan?" they'd ask. The first time I heard this one, I genuinely didn't know what they were talking about. "Huh?" I said. "You know, are you going to go drug free?" "Have you thought about a home birth?" "Are you using a doula?" *A doula?* I didn't even like the sound of that word. I immediately put it in the same mental category as "panties" and "ointment."

"I already know I'm having a C-section," I said, maybe a little too cheerfully.

You'd think I'd announced that I was having a C because I had tickets to Coachella, and there was no way mama was missing Wu Tang and Arcade Fire.

"*Really?*" they'd say, barely trying to hide their discomfort. "Don't you want to at least *try* for a vaginal birth?" Yes, women really say shit like this to other women. I wouldn't make it up.

I was pissed, but I have to admit that it did make me feel a little insecure. So I asked my obstetrician if there was any chance I could do this the old-fashioned way.

"No," she said. "You have scars on your uterus, and if you went into hard labor, your uterus could rupture. So even though there's only a very small chance of that happening—"

"Hold up," I said. "You had me at 'rupture.'"

I wasn't trying to be a hero or beat any odds; I just was trying to have a healthy baby. So I went ahead and had my C-section, went home three days later with a baby girl, and that was that. Did I complain about the pain just a little longer than necessary so I could get a refill of my Vicodin? Sure. I mean, have you met me?

After my surgeries and a first child delivered by C-section, you'd think I'd be well off the radar of the natural-childbirth commandos. And you'd be wrong. Some of them seemingly can't abide *any* obstacle to the vaginal birthing they feel is every woman's due. A few years later I was pregnant with twins when, in the last trimester, it became clear that because of complications, they would probably have to come out early. Not long after getting this stressful news flash, one of these Vaginistas saw fit to inform me that it was absolutely possible to deliver preemie twins naturally, because she herself had done it, and everything worked out fine. No medical degree, no obstetric research to back this up—just an apparent passion for the healing magic of the birth canal. I thanked her while backing away slowly and made a mental note to avoid that Whole Foods for a couple years.

My final adventure with this particular type of well-meaning zealot came about a year after my twins arrived and, after a nerve-wracking month in the NICU, came home tiny but healthy. After hearing of my experience with two C-sections, a woman suggested that, having been denied the "primal bonding" of natural birth, I might want to look into a ritual called "re-birthing" to make up for the bonding opportunity I'd clearly lost by not having pushed any of my three daughters out. She described a process of getting into a tub of warm water in the dark and letting your baby float around like they're in the womb before guiding them slowly out of the water and laying them on your chest. "First off," I said, "my oldest is four." "So?" she replied, clearly not hearing her own insanity. I couldn't help but imagine my foot bonding with the woman's ass.

I realize that not all women are like this. There are plenty of mothers who manage to maintain a supportive "to each her own" mentality no matter what type of birth they had. These are women I need to hang out with more often. But even though you can find judgmental beeyotches in either camp, it does seem that the "natural," "drug-free" extremist moms are the most competitive. I'm just saying, I've never witnessed a woman try to shame her friends into having a C-section! So why do certain women need to brag about their drug-free birth like it's a badge of honor? At what point did a "natural" childbirth become something to lord over another woman like a Chloé handbag or the square footage of your house? I honestly have no interest in how holistic your birth process was, okay? And on the flip side, it doesn't bother me, either. Although if you have a recipe for placenta tacos on your refrigerator I can pretty much guarantee we won't have a lot to talk about.

It wasn't all that long ago when all moms just did the full-on Betty Draper: put me out and wake me when I have a baby. Now you have to give birth in a tree house, doing downward-facing dog, while chanting warrior affirmations, to feel like you truly had a birth experience. It's hard to remain immune when our culture seems to increasingly fetishize the birth process.

So, yeah, when my sister-in-law told me how magical her birth experience was, I did feel a twinge of jealousy. And when I read statistics on C-sections in the news whose only function seems to be to give women another thing to judge themselves and each other for, it hits a nerve. But I have three beautiful, healthy girls, and only the tiniest of scars on my bikini line to show for it.

And I love that scar. It's my battle wound and it shows me what *my* body is for. And that's the only thing that counts. Well, that and the fact that my vagina is still adorably girlish and I don't leak pee when I laugh. So I don't regret my C-sections. Not at all. On the downside, my recovery time was a bit longer since it is major surgery and not something to be taken lightly. But on the plus side? I got to avoid taking Lamaze class with a bunch of a-holes! It's all in how you look at it.

A Few Alternative Birth Methods
We Should Try Not to Make Fun Of

Water birth: This one is super trendy right now. This is where you imitate the womb situation by having your baby delivered into water. You can do this in a tub at a birthing center or even in your backyard swimming pool! But if you go the swimming-pool route, don't forget to reschedule the pool guy. Otherwise . . . awkward.

HypnoBirthing: This is where you use relaxation, visualization, and meditation techniques to reduce pain when you're going through labor. Sounds good, unless your hypnotist is Criss Angel. Then, creepy.

Birthing from Within: Apparently this is a method of giving birth as a rite of passage. The tagline on their website reads, "How am I experiencing the profound wonder of birth?" And someone is wearing war paint. This just can't be a good thing.

Birth swing: Get one of these installed and then prepare to give birth while suspended from your ceiling or hanging upside down. If you really want your child's first moments on earth to look like something off a Cirque du Soleil blooper reel, be my guest.

Silent birth: This one comes to us courtesy of Scientology. Katie Holmes did a silent birth, as did Kelly Preston, who is quoted as saying, "There's as little talking as possible, but you can still make natural noises like grunting and crying." Which I just did while reading that quote.

Lotus birth: This is where you don't cut the umbilical cord after your baby is born and you just leave it attached for a few days until it dries up and falls off on its own. Or . . . in a few years you end up walking your kid around by his or her umbilical cord like a leash.

Orgasmic birth: Be fucking serious. This is not a real thing and just goes to show you how out-there some people get. You don't hear anyone saying they had an orgasm having their spleen removed, do you?

Diary of a Trip to the Zoo

8:00 a.m. Wake up super excited to use my free passes for the zoo, if only to see the Asian elephant exhibit. Try to rally kids to my level of excitement. Fail.

8:30 Argue with kids about the value of a good breakfast, bringing up the excellent point that I don't want to start buying expensive snacks at the zoo as soon as we get there since it defeats the purpose of free passes.

9:00 Give five-minute warning that we are leaving for the zoo.

9:05 "Please put your shoes on."

9:06 "Please put your shoes on."

9:07 "Please put your shoes on."

9:08 "Put your shoes on."

9:09 "Put. Your. Shoes. On."

9:40 Leave for the zoo.

10:30 Arrive at the zoo with clenched jaw and sore neck from listening to kids argue about whether or not orangutans are monkeys. I settle the argument by letting them know orangutans are indeed monkeys. After Googling it in the parking lot I find out I'm wrong. Orangutans are apes. I do not share this.

10:45 After waiting in a long line to get into the zoo, realize passes are expired and we must pay full **price.**

10:48 Kids say they are starving. We head to the **nearest** snack stand.

10:55 Pay $67 for three hot dogs, one order of onion rings, a pretzel, and three lemonades. One $4 lemonade spills on the way to the table. Shed my first tear of the day.

11:20 Throw away most of the food and listen to kids yell that they want ice cream. Think about wanting a beer. Remember I don't drink anymore and shed a second tear. Begin to suspect this may have been a bad idea.

11:22 Head to flamingos. After making it about twenty feet, six-year-old claims she's too tired to walk. Carry her for two minutes before deciding that it would be best to rent a stroller. Other six-year-old doesn't want to walk either. Pay $11 for a double stroller.

11:35 Heave double stroller weighed down by the ninety-pound combined weight of two six-year-olds in the general uphill direction of the flamingos.

11:45 Stop at flamingos. Kids can't see through the fence. Suggest that getting out of the stroller might provide access to a better vantage point. Get met with dead stares.

11:47 Begin hyping the Elephants of Asia exhibit.

12:00 Attempt to bypass the insects due to intense dislike of bugs. Fail. Spend next ten long excruciating minutes in front of a Madagascar hissing cockroach. Find out against my will that female Madagascar cockroaches give birth to live young. Know in my heart of hearts that there won't be enough Tylenol PM in the world to help me sleep tonight.

12:15 Head in general direction of elephants, which seem to be at the farthest point of the zoo.

12:17 Kids spot playground and insist on stopping to play.

12:58 Explain that we really must move on to see some animals, since if the kids were just going to want to play on a playground for an hour we could have walked to the park.

1:15 Move at snail's pace toward elephants. Nine-year-old wants to stop and rest. Sit down on bench. Kids decide they are ready to go home.

1:25 Insist that we stop at bat-eared fox exhibit because we are going to see some goddamned real animals if it fucking kills us!

1:27 Start questioning parenting ability.

1:39 Generate a small amount of interest in stopping to see the apes.

1:50 Maneuver all kids out of stroller and through throngs of unruly kids and adults, and finally get them positioned right smack in front of the apes. Success. Feel secretly smug about being a great mom.

1:51 Look up at where people are pointing to see the biggest ape standing front and center furiously masturbating.

1:51:30 Remember thirty seconds too late that most apes, unlike humans, have zero sexual modesty. Begin trying to explain about how apes sometimes can get a very itchy penis.

1:52 Six-year-old wonders if ape's penis got poison ivy since it seems so extremely itchy.

2:00 Push on toward Asian elephants while answering question after question about itchy penises.

2:10 Promise ice cream just as soon as we see the elephants.

2:11 Stop at ice cream cart and spend $16 on four glorified Popsicles. Curse life.

2:20 Ask kids to please stop saying the word "penis."

2:30 Arrive at the elephants, which are all sleeping. Feel like crying. But then start joining children in yelling to elephants, "Wake up! Wake up, you lazy elephants! You have a job to do! You are asleep on the job!" Start giggling. When six-year-old yells, "Hey, they don't pay you the big bucks to lay around all day!" start laughing.

2:32 See elderly couple give kids and me a dirty look. Laugh harder. Think to self that some people take the zoo way too seriously.

2:40 Return the stroller.

2:45 Carry six-year-old through the parking lot because her "legs hurt from walking so much!"

3:00 Drive home while mentally tallying the cost of the day, which, including entrance, comes out to $157. Look in rearview mirror and see two out of three kids fast asleep, one of whom is covered in chocolate Popsicle. Admit to self that, in the end, it actually was totally worth it.

Let Them Eat Cake

Here's something people should have told us about kids before we had them: you have to feed them, like, almost every day. It's seriously oppressive. And figuring out which foods are healthy yet easy to prepare, but that your kids will actually eat, is one of the biggest hurdles in parenting. Well, that and getting through an entire episode of *Caillou*.

Full disclosure right out of the gate: I have a dark, sordid past when it comes to food. When I was a kid, "sugary" cereals were banned from our house. I had to make do with Cheerios, Corn Flakes, and the occasional box of Total. For flavor we would be forced to cut up a banana or sprinkle in raisins. Yeah, raisins. Sit with that a minute. It wasn't a bragging point to possess the most regular bowels in the fifth grade.

The more I begged for the stuff the other kids took for granted, the more I was lectured on the evils of sugar. You would've thought my mother found out Kellogg's was dusting Froot Loops with just a dash of Agent Orange. Of course, this only added to the allure. I remember staring longingly at the boxes of Count Chocula on the grocery store shelf (while my mom reached right past it to grab for a box of something with a picture of bran, molasses, and pinecones on the front), thinking, *God, what I wouldn't do for ten minutes of alone time with you, Count Choccy! I want to eat you so hard!*

It's true: I spent the better part of my childhood having kinky fantasies involving breakfast cereals that contained more than three grams of sugar per serving. Since they were the forbidden fruit—or more accurately, fruity pebbles—it was almost inevitable that by the time I was living on my own, I was buying Cap'n Crunch in bulk and could eat an entire box in one sitting. Was I also stoned? Yes, but I'm choosing not to focus on that aspect of it.

I'm sure my mother was doing what she felt was best, trying to ensure that I started my day with a healthy breakfast and that my taste buds didn't need food to be overprocessed and insanely sweet in order to taste good. But, in actuality, what it did was give a simple box of cereal *crazy superpowers.*

Now that I'm the mom, I refuse to play that game. I attempt to present all food in a neutral way—no heroes or villains on our shelves. I do buy Kix, but there is also always a box of Lucky Charms in my pantry. And none of my kids care about it all that much. Especially after they've picked out all the marshmallows. Weird, huh?

The problem is it's difficult to try to keep that balanced attitude about what our kids eat when the world seems to be conspiring to make us feel crazy. The messaging starts even before we arrive! When my sister-in-law was pregnant, she came over to my house all panicked after her thirty-week checkup with her perinatologist. Everything had been fine with the baby's heart, lungs, and brain, but right toward the end of the appointment he blindsided her with a lecture on weight gain, despite the fact that her weight was within normal range.

"It's not about you, it's about the baby," he said. "You can give your unborn child the genes for obesity by eating sweets and high-calorie foods. But it's not too late to turn things around." She was horrified. And I was horrified for her! I wish I'd been there, because I would have said, "No, *you're* giving her fetus a teeny tiny eating disorder, asshole!" I think it took two Krispy Kreme donuts to help her calm down. The third one was for the baby, poor thing.

Is it any wonder that parents are becoming increasingly obsessed with every bite that goes into their kids' mouths? Exhibit A: the millions of mothers like me who think they can go on the culinary down-low, as recommended by books like *The Sneaky Chef* and *Deceptively Delicious*. I don't know a parent alive who hasn't bought one of these books in the hopes of tricking their kids into eating a pancake laced with spinach. Personally I've never seen this succeed on any kid in possession of working taste buds. Can you blame them though? Most of these recipes look pretty gross. I mean, chickpea brownies or avocado mousse, anyone? But even if you could successfully smuggle a quarter of a broccoli floret into a chocolate cake, who really wins here? Do you think you've kept beriberi at bay? Will it make the difference between your kid's making the Olympic team versus languishing in JV? Plus, all of this sneaking healthy stuff into our kids' food doesn't solve the problem, it creates a new one: it trumpets the message "brownie = good, broccoli = bad."

One of the basic problems is that kids are going to like what they're going to like regardless of how much we try to control it. Case in point: one of my daughters claims her favorite food is salad, and she once ordered fruit for dessert off of the kids' menu in a restaurant. And yes, the server looked at her like she was "special," but I internally high-fived myself for my awesome parenting skills. Then I remembered my older daughter refused to eat anything but bagels and cream cheese for three years straight. In that moment I realized that most often kids' palates and preferences are more nature than nurture, so you have to do your best with the taste buds you're dealt.

Don't get the wrong idea; I'm a fan of healthy eating. I'm not suggesting that kids should just be thrown in front of the TV with a big bag of Red Dye No. 3 for dinner. The goal is for all our kids to be healthy. I just want us to avoid driving ourselves crazy and giving our kids a lifelong complex if they don't eat what we want them to all the time.

So how do you maintain balance? Well, first you have to ask yourself if you're out of balance.

Have you ever packed your kid's school snack with homemade buckwheat flaxseed crackers that you made from scratch? Did you ditch your Starbucks fix in favor of starting every day off with an organic strawberry-açai almond milk with a shot of kale smoothie as a chaser? If you as much as smell the aroma of McDonald's fries, do you break into a cold sweat, call in sick to work, and start a detoxing cleanse stat? If any of these sound like you, you may be a health food junkie. This is a real thing with an actual name;

it's called orthorexia and it's defined as an obsession with healthy eating. I'm not making this shit up either. It was even on the *Today* show. Apparently thousands of people suffer with this disorder and it's growing rapidly. Personally, I blame Gwyneth Paltrow.

Look, we can all agree that pesticides are not a helpful part of our kids' diets, and I'm quite sure cutting down on the trans fats and partially hydrogenated oils is a big move in the right direction. But "everything in moderation" is a good policy too. If you read every single study you see in your morning news feed, I guarantee you will never again enjoy eating anything. To prove this theory, I just Googled "strawberries bad for you" and the first result was an article called "The Dark Side of Strawberries." Those bad boys may look like a sweet little mouthful of antioxidants, but apparently a nonorganic one is covered with thirteen different pesticides. Oh yeah. Also, according to a recent report, brown rice is now thought to contain high levels of arsenic—as if you needed another reason to avoid brown rice besides its tasting like nature's packing material.

Look, I'm aware of the dangers in a lot of our foods and I have probably drunk the Kool-Aid applauding organic fruits and veggies, avoiding plastic in the microwave, and opting for hormone-free milk and chicken. I also buy wheat bread even though we all know unless your bread is sprouting like a rotten potato, it may as well be white. So really, the bread thing is just mental. But I have to keep it realistic. I'm not filling my fair-trade, organic-cotton, reusable tote bag with a damn peace sign on it with groceries from Whole Foods. If I did, I'd have to take out a second mortgage on my house.

You aren't a shitty mom if you shop at the grocery store.

Unfortunately, there are some parents out there who take a far different approach and, in the process, often make it harder for the rest of us. Have you ever encountered a judgy snack mom, the one who has a better, farmer's-market-based option for every snack you bring to a play-date? She's fond of saying things like, "Oh, you know Whole Foods makes an all-natural version of that cheese and those crackers. That processed cheddar is so unhealthy." Or "Here, try some of these organic gummi bear substitutes; they're made from quinoa!" Let's all agree that while processed cheese may be questionable, *gummi bears should not be organic! It's against the laws of nature!* We need to draw the line on healthy eating somewhere, and I pick here!

While those moms are extreme, others are downright evangelical.

Have you made your kid abandon gluten, denying him the heavenly healing powers of a warm dinner roll slathered with butter? Must your child renounce complex carbs? Are they, God forbid, a *vegan*? If the answer to any of those questions is yes, then I just want to warn you that you are not setting your kids up for normal life in the real world. If *you* want to be gluten-free, do an eighty-day beet juice cleanse, or eat like a caveman for a year, then that's between you and your Facebook feed (actually, please stop posting that shit on your Facebook feed). But unless your child has celiac disease or another medical reason for excluding such a bready, delicious part of a balanced diet, there really is no good reason that they can't have gluten.

While most of us aren't nut-job extremists, we could all use a reminder sometimes about how important it is to maintain a balanced attitude about food. Our relationship with our children depends on it.

My daughter told me about a friend of hers at school who said, "My mom thinks I'm a vegetarian but when I'm at school I sneak and eat meat." My daughter asked her, "Why don't you just tell your mom that you don't want to be a vegetarian?" She replied, "Because my mom would be disappointed." This bummed me out on a couple of levels— that this girl couldn't be honest with her mom, but more importantly that she was having to rely on an elementary school cafeteria to get her daily meat fix. I wanted to kidnap this kid and take her out with our family for a juicy prime rib dinner. But unfortunately there are some pesky laws against that. In the end I settled for a compromise and invited her over for a big bowl of Lucky Charms, and left the organic jerky in plain sight.

They Can't All Be Gifted

If there's one topic that I think needs to be retired from all momversations, it's the gifted talk. When did "gifted" become the "it" label for our kids? It seems like I am constantly hearing about someone whose kid has just been tested for gifted, someone whose kid is about to be tested for gifted, or someone whose kid is starting fires ("I think maybe he's just gifted!").

We've all been around that one parent who is fixated on the gifted thing and just can't stop bringing it up every time you speak to them, right?

You: Will we see you at gymnastics after kindergarten?
Mom of Potentially Gifted Child: Oooh, no. We have gifted testing next month.

You: Wait, I'm talking about today.

MOPGC: I know. Can't do it. We have to study.

You: I didn't know you could study for a gifted test. Isn't it like an IQ test?

MOPGC: Yes, but gifted kids are notoriously terrible at testing. That's one of the ways you know they're gifted.

You: I don't get it.

MOPGC: Maybe that's because your kid's not gifted.

This mania seems to be starting earlier and earlier, too. I had a woman once ask whether my kid's preschool catered to gifted kids. Apparently she needed a place that could accommodate her daughter's "advanced love of butterflies." For a second I laughed, but then of course I immediately wondered if there was anything wrong with my daughter. She too loved butterflies, but her love was rudimentary at best. I mean, she was into them, but she wasn't *into* them. I started to question myself. But then I remembered that my daughter has an advanced love of cookies and I calmed right down. Seriously, my kid can probably name at least twenty-seven different brands of store-bought cookies. Although I don't know how much of that is being gifted and how much we can chalk up to excellent parenting.

Look, I get it. "Gifted" is a loaded term. It brings with it the connotation of "advanced" and "special," and unless your reason for having kids was strictly to have an extra hand with the plowing on the farm, I'm guessing you'd like to feel that your kid is special.

According to many experts though, in reality, gifted doesn't necessarily mean advanced. Many "gifted" kids are emotionally sensitive, perfectionistic overthinkers and underachievers who have trouble relating to their peers, and although they may read *Harry Potter* at six, they could easily suck in math. But still, even with the possible drawbacks, no one's exactly rooting for their kids to *not* be gifted, right? It's understandable! We're all looking for a leg up for our kids in life. But I'm here to tell you that the "gifted" label isn't necessarily a fast track to the Ivy League.

I was tested for the whole gifted thing back in the seventies and the label didn't do me any favors. The good news was it got me out of class once a week to do papier-mâché and learn three chords on the guitar. The bad news is that it set the table for my parents, future teachers, and guidance counselors to constantly let me know that I was "not working up to my potential." Also, my giftedness didn't score me any points with my manager at the Burger King I worked at for a few years. In fact, I'm not sure he even noticed! Which is odd because I rocked a fry machine like a vandal!

But still, some parents want to have their kids tested for giftedness because they want to be able to support their kids' intellectual growth and take advantage of any extra educational opportunities that might be available for kids who fall under the gifted category. And then others just want to be braggy bitches. You know who you are!

So go ahead and do the testing, but if your kid does turn out to be gifted? *Keep that shit to yourself!* No need to be a human bumper sticker about it. Simmer down with the humble-bragging—"It's so hard to find ways to challenge my kid because he's so gifted!" Keep that stuff between you and your BabyCenter message board.

Most importantly, if you decide to test your child, I think it's imperative not to let them know. What happens to the kids who are tested and turn out to just be normal, run-of-the-mill kids? How are you going to break it to them without giving them a stigma?

"Well, honey, you're gifted. To me." Which we all know really means, *Come on, your kid may not be gifted but he's not dumb.* "I'm sorry the rest of the world doesn't see it but *I* think you're above average."

In my opinion, getting tested for being gifted is a slippery slope. For instance, even if your kid does turn out to be gifted, are you then going to be worried that they aren't *highly gifted*?

I should point out here that that the term "highly gifted" gets thrown around a little too often for my taste these days. Everyone whose kid learns to read a little on the early side would like to believe their kid is some sort of wunderkind. Here, I'll help you determine whether or not your child is highly gifted: they're not. That shit is totally rare! I mean, how many of the kids who attend your neighborhood school wrote a symphony at eight years old like Mozart? How many could challenge Bobby Fischer at chess at thirteen? And even if you do have a baby genius on your hands, don't get too excited; sure, Beethoven was a prodigy, but you know who else was? Ted Kaczynski. The Unabomber. Yup, accepted into Harvard at sixteen . . . and a serial killer.

I have a friend whose daughter is highly gifted. Like, the real kind—the kind where she kinda sorta of taught herself to read when she was *two*. Taught herself. We're not talking about a Daryl Hannah–in–*Splash* situation where she watched a lot of TV and picked up the language. No, this kid just started looking at books and *reading*. It completely freaked her parents out. She had the vocabulary of an adult at the age of three but dumbed it down to talk to kids her own age, "so that they'd understand." You meet this little girl and you're like, *That right there is some spooky shit.* Well, as you can imagine, highly gifted kids aren't so spectacular at blending in and relating to their peers because of their genius IQ and all. Imagine how much fun Bill Gates isn't to sit around with and watch football. Exactly.

So my friend, trying to support her daughter's natural talents, sent her to a gifted-type school but realized very quickly that this was the wrong move. She and her husband figured out that the skill their kid really needed at six was to learn to be a friend. She'd have plenty of time to translate *Anna Karenina* from its native Russian into fourteen other languages just for a fun summer project at home— she didn't need to waste valuable macaroni-gluing, friendship-building, cupcake-eating time to do it.

As long as your kids are in a school that keeps them challenged, they're going to do fine. Anyway, whether or not your kids test gifted certainly doesn't guarantee they are headed for great achievement in life. I know some really smart people who are in their forties and still living with their parents while they wait to break out as a dubstep DJ, and I know some really average people who get to tell me what to do. So let's take the pressure down a notch on our kids and focus on the three H's: happy, healthy, and not on heroin. Now, there's some bragging rights!

The bottom line is we all want our kids to be successful in life, and the real key to success is perseverance, being goal oriented, and having a buttload of self-confidence. So for that reason, I'm not trying to raise little Einsteins, I'm trying to raise little Kardashians. Come on! Who has more cash?

The Tyranny of the Family Dinner

Fucking Olive Garden commercials have ruined family dinners for everyone. Those perky thirty-second TV spots give the impression that families enjoying their evening meal together are full of amusing, lively conversation; gentle ribbing; some warm remembrances of the old world from Uncle Zito; and maybe a few too many buttery garlic bread sticks. I don't think this gives an accurate portrayal of how family meals actually go down in the real world (besides the eating way too many bread sticks—that's pretty legit).

In my house growing up I can't remember a single dinner where one family member's supposedly innocent comment didn't cause another family member to storm off in tears mid-meatloaf. One night, a disagreement over the pronunciation of Ronald Reagan's name caused a battle royale. My stepfather pronounced Ronald Reagan's name Ronald Ree-gan. When I corrected him he tried to claim that he knew for a fact that Ronald Reagan's name could be pronounced either way. So I corrected his correction by saying that if the pronunciation of our president's name was such a free-for-all, then why did *no one else apart from him choose to exercise their right to pronounce it Ree-gan*? That argument lasted well into *Ray-gen*'s second term.

But even the meals that passed without high drama weren't exactly the magical bonding experiences we see depicted in movies and television. And yet, despite my less-than-fond personal memories of family mealtime, some new studies have been coming out telling us that regularly sitting down to meals as a family is critical to our kids' futures—that if you don't sit down with your kids for "family dinners" you are basically *killing their future*! A study out of Yale University claims that family mealtimes are associated with "such diverse outcomes as reduced risk for substance abuse, promotion of language development, academic achievement, and reduced risk for pediatric obesity." Great. So basically, if we don't sit down for dinner all together every night, our kids are going to turn into fat, mute, dumb drug addicts! In short, if your kids' dinner

comes from a drive-through window, their care
peak on the other side of one.

I just hope for my sake that "family mealtime
loosely defined as letting my kids eat a package of ciioco-
late-chip muffins and string cheese on their way to musical
theater practice. Does it count if they're sitting three across
the back row of the minivan and I'm fully engaging with
them through the rearview mirror? If not, I'm afraid we're
doomed.

Our whole family rarely sits down for dinner together
for several reasons: First off, kids are notorious for wanting to eat dinner at a truly uncivilized hour. I don't want
to eat chicken nuggets at five p.m. while watching *Bob the
Builder*; I want to eat Thai at nine with my husband while
watching *Mad Men*. And I want my kids to be sleeping. Call
me selfish, but that's a whole lot more relaxing. Speaking
of *Mad Men*, back in the sixties, "family mealtime" meant
enjoying a Swanson frozen Salisbury steak with peach cob-
bler in adjacent recliners while watching Ed Sullivan and
sipping scotch. Man, they don't call them the good old days
for nothin'! By the way, TV dinners were invented right
after World War II because after four years of driving rivets
into tanks and bombers, the gals finally had gotten butch
enough to demand a way to put family dinner on the table

without starting at dawn. If we go back on that, it's sort of like that whole war was really for nothing, right?

Another big issue I have is this: what sort of no-extra-curricular-activities-chasing, no-homework-having, no-TV-watching utopia are these family meal eaters living in? I mean, how are we supposed to have family dinners every single night if our kids are busy doing a bunch of impressive crap to look good on their college applications so they can get into Yale and turn out more studies that reveal what neglectful dopes their parents are?

If I tried to corral my kids for a sit-down meal around six p.m., what would happen to homework, tennis lessons, *Oklahoma!* practice, and karate? I mean, my kids are often busy during your standard dinnertime. Well, according to another really irritating article I skimmed in *Psychology Today*, these reasons are just excuses. Behold:

> *Janet and Sam had a problem. Their four busy children had tons of afterschool activities, from basketball, to Model UN, to cheerleading. When it was time for dinner, they were lucky to have a single child at the table. So, Janet made a decision. She woke up at 4:30 every morning and prepared dinner for breakfast! Gone were eggs and toast; and in came*

steak, veggies, and salad. The kids loved it. They
were together; they bonded and told stories—all
while half-asleep. It made memories that will last
a lifetime. Not all of us are as determined as Janet,
but her emphasis on meals together is correct.

According to the article, one year later, Janet went on to brutally murder her entire family. They traced her by following the trail of blood and arugula. Please don't fact-check me on this.

The good news is that for every article that will have you dipping into your kid's Adderall, you can easily find another one to balance it out. The *New York Times* came out with a piece called "Is the Family Dinner Overrated?" that basically debunked the other ones. Its not-so-shocking conclusion? Yes. Yes it is: "Our findings suggest that the effects of family dinners on children depend on the extent to which parents use the time to engage with their children and learn about their day-to-day lives." They go on to say that it's more about finding ways to connect with your kid than sitting down to a meal seven nights a week that will keep them off the chronic and out of the pokey.

I'm not saying you *shouldn't* try to have dinner with your family. Do I sometimes sit down with the kids for a meal?

Sure. But I keep my expectations low. Mealtime with young kids is not exactly packed with intrigue. My children's conversations are limited to such scintillating topics as "Why are you calling it Taco Tuesday when it's Friday?"; "Why can't I eat soup with a fork since she's doing it?" (that conversational gem is followed by twenty minutes of crying); and, naturally, "Who farted?" But, on the bright side, at least I never get judged for not being up on current events.

So sure, family dinners are a great way to spend time together and be, like, close as a family unit or whatevs. But if you're lazy like me, you can still find some other great ways to bond. A few nights ago, all three of my kids danced around the living room naked to LMFAO's "Sexy and I Know It"—until the UPS truck dropped off a package. There's nothing like impromptu and interrupted nudity to bring a family together. So hey, Yale University, put that in your pipe and smoke it!

Lulu Le'Mom:
In Defense of Yoga Pants

— - -- - -- -- - -- - -

I've let myself go a little bit, and I'm ready to own it and I want the world to own it too! I'm a mom. If you couldn't tell by my yoga pants, my ride would totally give it away. Yeah, I drive a minivan, bitches! When you're pregnant you don't think it's going to happen to you—that transformation from hip, happening woman who's not opposed to trying new restaurants, to suburban frump-a-lump: a woman with ill-fitting bras who may or may not cut her own bangs. I know, right? Who would ever cut her own bangs besides a fifteen-year-old in the throes of PMS crying to a Selena Gomez video? A mom, that's who: a mom who hasn't seen her colorist in five years and whose most recent haircut was courtesy of Fantastic Sams. Hey, they didn't do a bad job on my kids and I was already sitting there! Don't judge!

No one sees the metamorphosis coming. It's sort of the reverse of a caterpillar turning into a butterfly: it's the butterfly who starts out in skinny jeans and Jimmy Choos and ends up in sweats and shower shoes. But where's the Eric Carle book about that? Instead of *The Very Hungry Caterpillar* it would be called *The Not Actually Hungry Mom of a Toddler Who's Eating Her Feelings*. I'd totally read that book.

Look, there are going to be a lot of Internet articles telling you that taking care of yourself is super important to your self-esteem and that you need to take time to do you blah blah blah. But we all know that you're not going to follow that advice. Why? Because it actually steals more of your time and energy to go through the trouble of finding a sitter while you go get your hair cut—or, God forbid, tow your kids along with you—than to just let that shit grow and stick it in a ponytail.

It's not that I'm actively against taking time for yourself. Of course I understand that we moms spend most of our time caring for, listening to, thinking about, and generally putting first other mini-people. I'm just saying that for me, if I'm going to pay a babysitter, I'm not going to waste that time sitting in a hair salon reading *Us Weekly*, I'm going to go out with my friends or actually spend time with my husband that doesn't involve arguing with him about why there are scrambled eggs under the couch cushions when I specifically made a rule that the kids are not allowed to eat in the living room. Ain't nobody got time for that.

Remember that "No Excuse" mom, Maria Kang? The one who posted a picture of herself to Facebook posing in an itty-bitty red sports bra and boy shorts showing off rock-hard abs, surrounded by three little kids, and captioned it, "What's Your Excuse?" Yeah, well when that photo went viral there was quite a bit of backlash against her due to moms feeling like, *Fuck that! Yeah, we have excuses! Quite a few!* Plenty of moms felt that Maria was shaming them by setting an unrealistic expectation that they should be able to look like some sort of professional-wrestling ring girl four months postpartum.

I have to admit I found the whole thing pretty irritating myself. It's just not realistic for a lot of us. Here's a quote from Maria Kang's website: "What is a No Excuse Mom? She's a mom who makes no excuses for making her health a priority. She's someone who prioritizes her health, her family's health and understands the ripple effect their role plays in the health of their community." Okay, hold up, Maria; now I'm responsible for the health of my entire community? Can you get your foot off of my back? Oh, it gets worse: "These moms chose to transform their lives by consciously deciding every day that their health was worth it. When they were tired they trained. When they were lost for time to exercise, they found the time. When they were busy, they purposefully planned and prepared their daily goals and meals to coincide with what they wanted out of life."

Luckily, that paragraph was just long enough for me to eat a sleeve of Thin Mints and doze off for a much-needed thirty seconds. *It's ridiculous.* Look, before #TeamMaria freaks out on me, I'm not saying that as soon as we pop out a shortie we should commit to a life of muumuus and Wendy's; I'm not in favor of abandoning your health, and I'm certainly not advocating for an all-sugar lifestyle where your diet delivery service brings cookie dough for breakfast, churros for lunch, and cotton candy for dinner (although now that I've written it down, someone's going to steal this idea and make a boatload of money off of it). I'm simply pointing out that some stuff, such as washboard abs and a consistently hairless bikini line, is going to fall by the wayside. And that's okay! You are far from alone and should not be required to add "didn't run a marathon" to your already-long list of things that make you feel guilty for letting shit fall apart a little.

It's okay to relax our standards.

So I wear yoga pants every day, and I've never actually done yoga. Shut up. The problem is I have a little bit of a muffin top and jeans dig into my sides, so it's either yoga pants or I'm going prematurely into elastic waistbands. I'm not ashamed either, although truth be told I'm hoping people assume that I have plenty of pairs of jeans that I could wear if I *chose* to but that I constantly rotate Old Navy yoga pants because I'm on my way to the gym! And really, I often *am* on my way to the gym. I may not get there until forty-eight hours later, but I'm still on my way, so *get over it!*

The main downside of wearing exercise pants exclusively is that it's very difficult to look put together. I can't exactly dress them up with dangling earrings or a statement necklace, and really, what shoes are you going to wear besides flip-flops? So if I'm in yoga pants and flip-flops it just seems awkward to have a face full of makeup. And if I have no makeup on, then what good does it do for me to make an effort with my hair? And if I'm not going to blow-dry my hair, then I figure I may as well shower at night and just sleep on it wet, right? And this is how I've come to resemble a borderline vagrant three-quarters of the time. And sure, it's sad that I've gotten used to not looking presentable, but it's not the end of the world.

Recently, I had an actual reason to put on mascara and

do my hair. When I later ran my daughters to swimming lessons, the instructors freaked out at the sight of me looking the way other women look on a normal day. "Wow, you look so fancy! Where are you going?"

And that's when I realized just how far down the "no effort" rabbit hole I'd fallen. But one of my "excuses" is that I work freelance more or less from home; the only time I have for face time with other people is when I'm shuttling my kids to and from activities or when I occasionally meet another mom for coffee. When I think about my friends who have jobs where they have to actually go in to work and be around other people every day, I can't help but wonder how the hell they find the prep time required to look presentable.

But guess what! I stumbled upon some good news! There's a new brand of yoga pants designed to look like dress pants! A company called Betabrand is advertising them all over Facebook and these bitches are about to catch on like wildfire, because *hi, comfy pants that you can wear to the office*! Of course anytime life is made easier for women, some assholes are going to get bent out of shape (in which case I recommend stretchy work pants, which are perfect for bending!). Yeah, there are some haters (see Internet comments, bloggers, Fox News) who worry that we moms have gotten so damn lazy that it's now to the point where we can't even be bothered to put on pants that involve a zipper. They question how far away we are from wearing PajamaJeans to argue a case in front of the Supreme Court or Jeggings to our senatorial debate. I don't know. I guess anything's possible. I mean, dare to dream, right? If someone designs a Snuggie—that blanket-with-sleeves phenomenon with the remote control in the pocket—that you can wear to the office, count me in as your first customer! Hey, Betabrand, get on that, would you? And, by the way, if you are a mom and you are running for mayor, can you please make work yoga pants part of your platform? Thanks!

Seriously, let's all stop leaning in so much and lean out! Let's start a movement! I'm calling on all female celebrities to slow down on taking off the baby weight. Get off Weight Watchers and into a box of Ritz crackers! It's okay to look like you have a baby! I want to collectively lower our standards, but I can't do it alone. I'm only one woman. One woman with a muffin top in yoga pants. Won't you join me?

Kids' Art: They're Not All Picassos

There's no doubt that the first time your preschooler comes home from school with art, there will be excitement all around. You'll look at a piece of paper with a few blobs of color and squeal with delight! I mean, how did those little hands that were, until recently, barely capable of keeping a pacifier in their mouth create this masterpiece? And with each new finger painting, you'll be convinced you have a tiny Kandinsky on your hands. "This was no random swirling of colors," you'll tell everyone from your spouse to the guy who's just trying to sell you life insurance. "Don't you see how she made use of the negative space? Such an eye for composition!" People will roll their eyes, but you won't notice. After all, you pay a shitload of tuition at this preschool! They'd better be teaching something!

Soon your refrigerator will be covered with "master-pieces," many of which are basically a sheet of black construction paper that is almost completely blank save for a single rigatoni noodle and some dried glue. In a few months your collection will have spilled over from the fridge to take up valuable wall space. It can get really out of control really fast. One day you'll look on your living room wall and realize that that picture you put in a frame? It's actually a kids' menu from IHOP with a few scribbles on it.

Now you have a problem.

Kids are not really artists, yet most of us parents don't know when to stop treating every stick figure as if it were Picasso. I put a lot of the blame for this phenomenon on the shit show that is modern art. I mean, just think about modern art for a minute. Okay, that's long enough. Seriously, modern art is ridiculous. There's a reason that a lot of parents are deluded into thinking that their kid's splotch of blue paint had thought behind it; it's because at some point they saw something similar hanging in a museum of modern art, and thus started wondering if their kid is a genius.

Look, if you've felt that way, you're not alone. Remember that four-year-old who got her own show at a Chelsea art gallery? Well, I don't know for sure whether she was really good or if most modern art is just really bad, but no matter; that kid combined the right colors or her fingers made some lucky swirls, and suddenly people wanted to pay thirty grand to put that crap on their walls.

The truth is, that is never going to happen to you or your offspring. But if you consider a piece of your child's work to look a little exceptional, I say stick it in an expensive frame. Even the most experienced art critic may mistake your two-year-old's periwinkle crayon creation for postwar European art.

You can't save everything, though. No matter how much our children want us to celebrate each pencil doodle and clay "coaster" they make, we need to toss most of it if we are to keep our sanity. I'm guilty of keeping too much stuff myself. Up on my office shelf sits a mug that says "I Love Mommy" on it, drawn in marker. It's filled with old tissue paper and a pipe-cleaner flower. Did the teacher have to help her spell "Mommy"? Sure. Did the teacher also help her *write* "Mommy"? Maybe. Did the teacher actually *do* the writing? Yes! Whatever. You win. But she was only four. She wasn't supposed to be able to write yet, okay? (See "They Can't All Be Gifted," page 43). Lay off. The point is, it was made for me and I'm not letting it go. And that's okay. There will be drawings and mugs and handprints that you won't be able to part with that will forever take up space in your garage.

But what about the rest of it? What about the piles and piles of drawings and paintings that are everywhere? Is it okay to throw them out? Yes. Absolutely. Not only is it okay, it's necessary.

What's the upside to keeping all your kid's art? Are they going to open up a museum and be the curator? Are they going to spend years looking through dusty old boxes in the attic that contain over eighty thousand pieces of almost-blank paper? And really, if later on in life you find it necessary to show your child that you saved every single one of their scribbly drawings in order to prove that they were loved, it's safe to say that something went very wrong in your parenting.

Okay, so we've established that you don't need 99 percent of it; now what? Well, the best thing to do is gather it all together and make a small pile of the pieces you want to keep. And then make it smaller! Even smaller! That paper that your son splashed a few different colors of paint over? It's not a Jackson Pollock, it's a mess. Get rid of it. Be ruthless. Save only a few things from each era: the scribbles, the people with weird mouths and no feet, the houses (the many, many, many houses), the mermaids, the policemen, and a couple of rainbows if you're feeling generous.

When you've put a few away, gather the rest of them together, and then remove them from the house after all the children are in bed asleep. *This is important.* You'll need to sneak them out under cloak of darkness, because under no circumstance do you want to be seen. You can't have witnesses. If anyone sees you, you must kill them.

Don't make the mistake of tossing anything your kids have made into the trash, because kids can sniff out their stuff in the trash like dogs can sniff out an old tampon. And the results can be just as disastrous.

What if you do get caught? What happens if your child finds the "drawing" of the boat they did completely in yellow marker that so barely showed up on the page it may as well have been done in invisible ink? I mean, come on, how were you supposed to know that was a boat and not an old, slightly yellowish sheet of paper? There's an opportunity for a real teachable moment here: you can sit your child down and explain to them that although you appreciate all of their creativity, not everything they do needs a place on the wall or fridge to prove its worthiness, and that sometimes we have to make room for the next amazing piece of art.

Or you can do what I do and act like someone fucked us all over! Scream, "Oh my God! How did this happen? This wasn't supposed to be in the trash!" Blame the housekeeper. If your child brings up the point that you don't have a housekeeper, tell them that you just hired one! Another viable option: blame Dad. Always blame Dad. Then pull it out of the garbage, straighten it out as best you can, and tack that sucker right up on the wall, 'cause you're screwed. And by the way, that one's staying up there for the next few years at least.

The Joy of Quitting

--- -- -- -- -- -- -- -

*You've got to know when to hold 'em,
know when to fold 'em.*

—*Kenny Rogers*

So your eight-year-old son has been rocking it on the basketball court since he was four, but suddenly he's decided it's not fun anymore. The kid used to love basketball! Now you have to practically push him out the door. Finally you yell, "Do you even *want* to play basketball?" And he shrugs his shoulders and says, "Not really." *Not really?* You think about all the time and energy you've sunk into this: bringing sliced watermelon and gluten-free crackers for the entire team when you have snack duty, learning all the stupid rules so you can coach the team when the real coach is too hungover, driving your son and his three tons of equipment to and from the games and practices in your *stupid fucking Honda Odyssey*, not to mention the money you've spent on crap so he could practice at home—including an adjustable basketball hoop that cost 195 bucks plus shipping and took your husband fourteen hours and one sprained finger to put together! Damn it, you've got way too much skin in the game to let that little deserter walk away now! Instinctively, you go all Vince Lombardi on his ass and yell, "Winners never quit, and quitters never win!"

You know what? Let him quit. Yes, I said that. Let. Him. Quit. Quitting is totally underrated if you ask me. And you did ask me. You're reading my book, aren't you?

I myself am really good at quitting. I'm a champion quitter. If quitting were an Olympic sport I'd definitely medal. Then again, I started quitting really early, and I never quit quitting. As a kid I quit guitar lessons because I hated to practice, I quit swim team (the water was always criminally cold, and the chlorine gave me an Afro), and volleyball (no reason). When I got older I raised my quitting game to relationships that weren't working and jobs I didn't like. After all my earlier practice I could now quit with some real panache: I once stormed out of my waitressing job at Joy of the Wok in a blaze of glory, with all of the customers' checks still in my apron, because the manager was coked up and harassing me. Yes, I took a stand for service-industry women the world over. Or maybe I just wanted to go home, wash off the smell of soy sauce, and watch *The X-Files*. I'm not super clear on the details, but they aren't important; what is important is that I'm in favor of quitting if you know you would be happier not doing the thing you're doing, and I've never regretted any of those decisions.

Years ago, I broke up with a boyfriend because I found out he owned a fanny pack. Something at a very base level of my being knew that I couldn't commit my life to this type of person. A person who wears a fanny pack is a person who is always up for a hike; it's someone who says things like "Let's get the gang together to grill some dogs and drink brewskis"; it's a person who is definitely going to want to show you his skydiving video; it's someone who refers to the Dave Matthews Band as "DMB." Bottom line: it's someone who's not for me. And if I hadn't quit that relationship, I wouldn't have ended up with my husband, who despises hiking as much as I do. I never would have been available for the person who is perfect for me.*

I honestly believe that being able to walk away from something that's not working is a real strength—although I

---

*Full disclosure: My husband claims he despises hiking as much as I do. But on multiple occasions snooping through his old photo albums, I've come across a suspicious number of pictures of him hiking with exes. I also found a skydiving video.

wouldn't necessarily lead with it on a job interview: "What's my greatest strength? Hmmm . . . I guess I'd have to say my greatest strength is that I'm not afraid to quit a job at the spur of the moment for another job with fewer hours." You might want to stick with the whole "I'm too much of a perfectionist" or "Sometimes I just care too much" bullshit, just to be on the safe side.

Look, I get that we're talking about our kids here, and letting kids quit may not be the right move in every situation. Sometimes if your kid wants to stop doing something you have to ask yourself why. If the reason is that they are temporarily bored, or they're feeling challenged and it's made them uncomfortable, then by all means, try to get them to see it through, or at least ride out the rough patch. Come on, I'm all about character building as much as the next mom!

Case in point: When one of my twins was five she was in an adorable, fun little production of *Annie*, playing Rooster, Miss Hannigan's grifter brother. A few rehearsals before the performance, my kid decided she was done. She cried and said she didn't want to go anymore. And it gave me pause. I didn't want to force her, but, on the other hand, I suspected she was just a bit nervous, so even though there was another kid who could've stepped into her role (it was only a few lines, people), we made her see it all the way through. We wanted her to feel a sense of accomplishment and know that she could do it even if she was scared. And guess what? She killed it! In fact, her performance was so nuanced, sublime, and honest that an agent who happened to be in the audience signed her, and within a few months she was reprising the role of Rooster on Broadway. *Or* after we forced her to go to her last few rehearsals, she made it through her little play without incident and then promptly retired from the theater. Which was fine by us.

But maybe your kid isn't experiencing nerves or a little rough patch; maybe your kid is just not that into it. At that point you need to ask yourself, "What's the endgame?" You can force your six-foot-four fourteen-year-old to shoot a thousand jump shots a night and spend his summers at basketball clinics, but if that's not his idea, you can pretty much give up on the vision of the house he'll be buying you with his signing bonus. And your nine-year-old who would rather play with her friends than ice-skate five days a week, two hours a day, in order to compete on a national level isn't headed for Olympic glory, but if you force her to keep it up, she is probably headed for an eating disorder and early arthritis.

Keep in mind that if kids are actually into what they're doing, they are very often self-motivated. How many rock stars do you know who were forced to practice the guitar for forty-five minutes a day against their will? No way. They are way more likely to have blown off their homework on a daily basis because they were too busy smoking pot and jamming in their basements. I would bet most rock stars had a parent who was threatening to break their damn guitar if they didn't stop being so hyperfocused on it and start paying some goddamn attention in class. Then again, for every Eddie Van Halen, there are probably a shit-ton of unemployed forty-five-year-old dudes who are still smoking pot and refusing to move out of the basement because they're "artists."

But sometimes, even though it's crystal clear your kid doesn't want to do something anymore, and even though you know there's no real future in it for them, you may still have trouble letting them give it up, possibly because *you're the one who wants to do it* and you're living through your kid.

I have a friend whose daughter *really* wanted to quit playing soccer after a few years, because she didn't love it nearly as much as she loved to sing. But she couldn't quit, because soccer was her dad's first love. In fact, he's one of those insane soccer fans who thinks nothing of going to a

California pub at four a.m. to see his favorite English team play on a live satellite feed along with a bunch of other equally obsessed fans. Naturally, he was also his daughter's team coach.

When my daughter quit playing soccer, my friend said, "Dude! You're so lucky! My daughter can't quit! My husband's way too into it! What would he do if he couldn't coach them?" But, luckily, a season later, he came up with a great solution. He joined his own adult team and plays weekly. So now instead of screaming at refs while standing on the sideline, he gets great exercise running after the ball, screaming at the refs from midfield. Another plus: he can go drinking with his bros after the games. Taking an eight-year-old on a pub crawl after AYSO is largely frowned upon. Except maybe in Europe. But they also wear Speedos there, so they can't be trusted.

I myself have also learned from this. I finally quit trying to get my daughters to take gymnastics. They have no interest. But I do! I did gymnastics for a couple of years and was completely obsessed with it until I was forced to quit when my parents couldn't afford to send me anymore. And make no mistake: if I'd kept doing it, I'd totally have a bunch of gold medals around my neck right now—literally. At all times. Dropping by Starbucks? Medals on.

Mammogram? Medals on; just slide 'em to the side. But I digress . . .

One of the biggest problems with not letting kids quit things they're not interested in is that they may become afraid to try anything new, for fear they'll be stuck committing to it forever, forcing them to fake their own death just to get out of playing the oboe. It doesn't have to be this way.

You should treat choosing a sport or extracurricular activity for your children like dating. Before you rush into anything, look at some pictures with your kids of the sport or activity on a website and read a description to determine if there's an attraction there; if you like what you see, maybe go on the equivalent of a coffee date. You know, try out a free class, no expectations. If your kid feels pressured by the instructor or coach to sign up right away for more lessons or join the team, let them know that your child just got out of a serious relationship with another sport and isn't sure she's ready to "buy the uniform." She's playing the field right now. If your child gets interested and wants to take things to the next level, just go slow. And if on the other hand they decide it's not for them, consider it a win for your wallet! And your time!

So all of that said, don't worry if you feel like you're raising a quitter. It's a perfectly normal part of development and lets them know that life is full of tough choices and decisions. And, on the plus side, in twenty years they'll know exactly how to quit their two-pack-a-day smoking habit.

My Daughter's Imaginary Friend Is an Asshole

For the record, I don't have any problem with kids having imaginary friends. In fact, I've read that imaginary friends are quite common, especially among children who are bright, creative, and . . . well . . . imaginative. I had always assumed that imaginary friends by nature would be pretty fun and low maintenance as companions go—not needing much in the way of snacks and pretty much game to go anywhere your kid wants to go. I figured they were like having a sibling minus the endless, aggravating bickering. But when my older daughter was four she began a friendship with an imaginary friend named Angeli (still not 100 percent sure on the spelling) who, I don't mind saying, was kind of a bitch.

Oh sure, Angeli started out sweet and charming. She sucked my daughter in with her enthusiasm for playing princess or riding next to her in the car (she didn't have to sit in a booster seat). She kept my daughter company at Trader Joe's, sitting in the basket while my kid sat in the front of the cart, twisting herself all the way around to better hear Angeli's ice-cream flavor requests in the frozen-food aisle. But just like in every Lifetime movie, the relationship slowly turned abusive.

Turns out, Angeli? Not much of an angel. The signs that things were beginning to sour were subtle but typical of how these things go. First, Angeli started to make little controlling comments about what my daughter was wearing.

We were driving in the car when my daughter said, "Mom. I need to tell you something. Angeli doesn't like it when I wear long sleeves."

"Why not?" I asked.

"She never wears long sleeves because she doesn't like them."

"Huh. Well, that's fine for her, but why can't you wear them?"

"She doesn't want me to wear them because she says long sleeves are stupid."

"Honey, you can wear whatever you like. Angeli doesn't own you." *Jesus*, I thought. *It's hard enough to get a four-*

year-old dressed in the morning. I don't need Angeli weighing in on sleeve length. But why does Angeli care what sleeve length my kid wears anyway?

But that was only the beginning. Things slowly got worse.

A few weeks later, we were hanging out at home and out of nowhere my kid yells, "Mom, Angeli threw my Dora bathtub toy in the trash!"

"What are you talking about?" I was genuinely confused because, to be honest, I'd kind of completely forgotten about Angeli's existence.

"My toy that I was playing with. Angeli threw it away. She said it was an accident, but she really threw it away on purpose."

"Do you mean that *you* threw it away?" I asked, hoping to maybe throw in a quick reality check and make short work of "Angeli."

"No, Angeli didn't want me to play with it because she said it's for little, stupid babies."

"You can tell Angeli I said to suck it."

"What?"

"I said, tell Angeli 'tough luck.'"

This bizotch was really starting to work my nerves. And then, soon after the bathtub toy incident, Angeli got downright aggressive. We were on our way to Target and had *this* disturbing conversation: "Mom," piped up my daughter from the backseat, "Angeli said she's going to crack my head open."

"*What?* Why would she say that?" I was ready to turn the car around, head for the police station, and file an imaginary restraining order.

"Actually she didn't say it. Angeli's brother did. He's really mean." So her imaginary friend had a brother?

"Well, can Angeli talk to him and ask him not to threaten you with violence? Or do you want me to talk to him?" I glanced in the rearview mirror and she looked sad.

"Actually, Angeli doesn't want to be my friend anymore."

"I think it's probably for the best. Angeli sounds like a bad seed."

The next day I called a friend who is a therapist and asked how I could get rid of my daughter's imaginary frenemy. She told me that, on some level, my daughter knew her friend wasn't real. And she assured me that this was normal behavior, and more importantly that it was a phase my kid would soon grow out of. But in the meantime, she said to just go along with it and not make it a big deal.

I just hoped that perhaps Angeli meant what she said and was truly done with my daughter. But the very next day, while we were driving to the store, the bitch was back.

"Angeli is my friend again," my daughter said brightly, as if nothing had happened! "She wants me to come to a playdate at her house." That was not going to be happening. But I remembered what my therapist friend said and tried not to freak out.

"Doesn't she live with you at our house?"

"No. She lives in New York." Of course she did. Angeli was probably some spoiled rich kid living at the Plaza like Eloise or something. Her parents probably ignored her and just let her do whatever she wanted, coming and going as she pleased, flying around the country to visit her imaginary friends, charging her trips on their black Amex card. I bet her parents barely noticed, which might explain her manipulative, attention-seeking behavior.

"New York is pretty far. You'd have to take a plane to get there."

"Yes. I have to be on the plane for ten hundred days."

"So you're flying Southwest?"

"Huh?" I guess she was too young to appreciate airplane humor.

The subject was again dropped momentarily, but then while we were walking into the store, Angeli crossed the line.

"Mommy? I need to tell you something. Angeli kicked me really hard on my shoulder." Now I was pissed.

"Sweetie. Didn't you make Angeli up? Because when you make someone up, generally they shouldn't be abusing you. They should be buying you presents, making you laugh, and telling you how fabulous you are at all times. They should laugh at your jokes and make you feel like the smartest, most interesting person in the room! Trust me, before I met Daddy I had a lot of experience with this. My old therapist called it 'living in fantasy.' I preferred 'creative visualization.'"

"So can I go to Angeli's house?"

"Fine. As long as her asshole brother's not there."

I figured I'd have to let her go and make her own mistakes. But just to be safe, I signed her up for imaginary Krav Maga.

Cheating, Lying, and Stealing:
It's Normal, Yo!

Cheating

Have you ever had the disturbing thought that your child may be a sociopath? It's okay; we all have. Let's face it: kids are pretty dishonest by nature. I'm not sure if it's because they don't know better or because they think they're too cute to get caught, but most children at some point are going to cheat, lie, and steal and probably not feel bad about it. You shouldn't either. When my oldest daughter was around five, she was a major cheater. She openly cheated at Trouble, Hi Ho Cherry-O, Chutes and Ladders, Go Fish, and basically every game we played. I don't know if "cheating" is the right word—well, yeah, it actually is. She liked to change the rules in the middle of the game to suit her needs: did the spinner landing on the bird that eats two cherries from her bucket in Hi Ho Cherry-O set her back too much for her liking? Well, better spin again—that one was on the line. Did she land on the top of a chute that would send her sliding down to the beginning in Chutes and Ladders? Oh, that chute is broken, so weird! Does she have any sixes? Sorry, those aren't sixes, they're fours. Go fish.

We've all heard the phrase "it's not whether you win or lose, it's how you play the game," right? In the case of a lot of kids, it has nothing to do with how you play the game and everything to do with winning. Case in point: one night my kid wanted to play *one* game with me before stories (a famous stall tactic). I agreed to Candy Land, which I find to be dull, yes, but less egregious than, say, Pretty Pretty Princess, the game we usually played that made me want to stab myself out of sheer boredom. So Candy Land got set up and while I checked my phone for any texts that might have come in during the last thirty seconds, my daughter casually rustled through the cards looking for the ice-cream cone card. This was the card that, should you draw it, would put your plastic gingerbread man on the expressway all the way toward the end of the candy path, where it would then be poised to win the game in approximately five more turns. So my daughter sneaked the card onto the top of the pile when she thought I wasn't looking and then announced loudly that she was going first. I was actually impressed, thinking, *Hey, the kid's got strategy; she's thinking a couple of moves ahead. She's like the Bobby Fischer of board games.* But then she started pushing it.

"Mommy! Look! It's the ice-cream cone! I picked the ice-cream cone card first! Can you believe it?" Unfortunately, her acting skills were more Tyler Perry than Susan Sarandon.

"Wow, what a surprise," I said. Even though it *wasn't a surprise at all* considering the fact that *I'm not blind*!

And that's when I started to worry a bit. Here she was blatantly cheating and not looking the tiniest bit guilty about it! In fact, to the contrary, she looked downright pleased with herself! Was this conniving behavior normal, or was I raising a future congresswoman? Could I look forward to more deviant acts like, say, stealing term papers from the Internet and then proudly exclaiming, "Look, Mom, another A-plus! Can you believe it?" When she was eventually arrested for securities fraud and sentenced to ten years in prison, would I look back on this red flag from my seat in the back of the courtroom and think, *I should have known*?

According to the experts, it is totally normal for children at this age to be completely focused on winning, and when kids are completely focused on winning, they are more likely to cheat. But what can we do about it? Well, according to Parents.com, even when they're at the tender age of five, we're supposed to get tough. "Sit your child down and ask her why she cheated. Discuss the seriousness of what she did and ask her about the kinds of stresses and pressures that may have motivated her to cheat." Seriously? The stresses and pressures? Like what, learning to spot the difference between lowercase "b" and lowercase "d"? Having to choose between Froot Loops and Lucky Charms? Getting floss introduced into her bedtime routine?

I'll tell you what stresses *me* out: that kind of bullshit parenting advice.

The truth of the matter was, I admired my kid's desire to succeed and was happy to let her win. And more to the point, win as quickly as possible. And if I'm going to be really honest, I have been known to cheat in reverse. Ever played War with your kids? The card game where you each get half the deck of cards and then flip them over one at a time, and whoever's card is higher wins those cards? And then you keep going until someone either has all the cards or you pass away from natural causes? I have a tendency to throw the game. In fact, I'm not above similar deceptions to the "ice-cream card to the top of the pile" trick to help myself lose as quickly as possible.

But when my daughter zipped her game piece past Gumdrop Mountain and through Lollipop Woods singing, "I'm going to win! Look! The ice-cream cone space is almost at the end! I'm going to win!" I figured I should say *something*—if only to maintain my dignity.

So I went with, "You will get to win the game. But, on the other hand, the game will be over really fast."

"But on the *other* hand, you will lose," she said, looking at me like I was new to this planet. It was a little condescending.

"True. I guess you really like to win."

"I *love* to win," she said. This was a serious teachable moment staring me right in my face. But what the hell was I supposed to teach, exactly? The kid loves winning. I'm thinking the only problem is that she is going to be in for a rude awakening when she plays another kid who also loves to win and has little to no interest in letting her get away with cheating just to speed up the game and get back to more important issues, like Candy Crush.

"So, I don't mind if you win even if you didn't exactly do it fairly, but what's going to happen when you play with kids your own age? Sometimes you are going to lose." I braced myself for her to argue, since I'd just insinuated that she'd cheated.

"I know that, Mommy. It's okay. When I play games with my friends I don't cheat."

"Oh? And you're okay if you lose?"

"Sure. Sometimes I win and sometimes I lose. But when I play with grown-ups they don't mind if they lose and I really like to win, so it's okay." How can you argue with that kind of logic? With that reasoning, I'd love to see what she could do about health-care reform.

It took about thirty more seconds for her to finish me off. She got to beat the pants off me and I got to finish playing Candy Land in less than four minutes. I think anyone can see that is a win-win situation.

Lying

Rest assured, lying is extremely common in kids. Maybe even more common than cheating. We've all had our child's kindergarten teacher pull us aside at pickup to tell us that we "must be so happy to have our husband home from his clowning work with the traveling circus," right? No? Just me? Wow. That's hurtful. Well, despite your judgment, it is totally normal. Kids lie for a variety of reasons and very few of those reasons are nefarious. For one, little kids lie because they don't even quite know the difference between lying and telling the truth. Early on their life is filled with fantasies they believe to be true, such as Santa Claus, the Easter Bunny, and the Tooth Fairy (notice I capitalized Tooth Fairy—because, like God, the Tooth Fairy is still very much a real and venerable life force in my house). And who puts those fantasies in their head? *We* do. So when your child tries to convince you that the reason they took all the forks out of the kitchen is because they needed them to help run the jelly bean factory in their closet, how can we be mad when we've just convinced them that a fat guy with a sack of toys is going to be sliding down their chimney?

If we really want our kids to stop lying, unfortunately we're going to have to stop lying too, and that's not possible. We lie all the time. Sure, most of the lies are to avoid hurting someone's feelings or to get out of going to Pampered Chef parties, but they're still lies and our children learn from us. So if your kid is telling a lot of lies, before you get upset with them or seek professional help, first try to stop lying yourself. Not so easy, is it?

Stealing

But what about stealing, right? If your kid steals a pack of gum from CVS at six, does it mean they're headed for an orange jumpsuit at twenty-six? No. All kids attempt shoplifting at some point—I mean, unless they're a pussy.

When kids are under the age of five, and they take something from a store or preschool, you can't even call it stealing—they don't even have a concept of ownership yet. To them, taking something from a store or someone's house is simply sharing on a much larger stage. So when dealing with children under the age of, let's say, seven, don't go crazy, just let them know that the penny, shoelace, toilet plunger, Hot Wheels, or lipstick is not theirs and leave it at that. No need to punish them—unless you're in public and you want to seem like a responsible parent.

When kids are over seven and steal, simply telling them it's wrong is probably not gonna cut it. Because, duh, they know it's wrong, but it's still exciting to do! The bad news is that probably the only thing that will prevent them from living a life of crime is getting busted. But the good news is that pretty much every kid who steals at a young age is going to get caught. Let's face it, kids aren't exactly criminal masterminds—they aren't capable of pulling off any *Ocean's Eleven*–style shit.

Case in point: When I was around seven or eight, my friend and I used to walk to the Montgomery Ward store a few blocks from my house to browse. Yes, in those days we *walked*! To a store! *Alone!* We even crossed a four-lane street to get there! Hang up the phone. You can't report my parents for this; I believe the statute of limitations has passed.

Montgomery Ward had this amazing selection of penny candy, and often my friend and I would pocket a few pieces. I mean, not to blame the victim, but are you really going to put individually wrapped delicious caramels and butterscotches on display and not expect kids to take them? I'm sorry, but those Bit-O-Honeys were asking for it. One day, while the clerk was busy showing off the new Teflon nonstick pan technology one department over, my friend and I filled our pockets with candy and then nonchalantly walked outside to eat our loot on the way home. Just as we stepped outside the double doors into the sweet sunlight of freedom, a very large, less friendly-looking version of Kojak stopped us and asked us to empty our pockets. My friend burst into hysterical tears and I instantly peed my Toughskins.

We promptly handed over the candy, fully expecting to be arrested. I wondered what life would be like in jail. Could I take the Nancy Drew mystery I was in the middle of with me? Would I have to eat oatmeal? Or would they have those mini boxes of breakfast cereals like Frosted Flakes? To be honest, hanging out reading books with open access to sugary cereal didn't sound like the worst thing in the world.

But instead of arresting us, Kojak told us that he was going to let us go, but that he'd better not ever see us in the store again for the rest of our lives. I was flooded with relief, and I walked home with wet pants but no criminal record. Not only did I never step foot in Montgomery Ward again, but I never stole anything again, even later on when all my friends were doing it.

So far my children haven't tried to shoplift anything yet (that I know about), but I'm encouraging them to get on it soon! The clock's a tickin'. I need them to experiment with stealing while they're still too young to be charged with a felony. Look, I don't want to call myself a "hero"; I'm just a supportive mom doing her part to keep her kids from landing in the pokey.

Eff the Park

I hate the fucking park. Yeah, I said that. That happened. And guess what? I refuse to feel bad about it. I've taken my kids to the park a million times, I've put in the hours, I've *earned* my right to bitch. If you're a newbie mom, you might be thinking, *Whoa, calm down. What could be bad about letting the kids run around and play outside getting a little vitamin D while you chat with other moms and take advantage of all those photo ops? It's relaxing.* All I can say is that if you find the park relaxing, one of us isn't doing it right. And, trust me, I have more than enough photos of my kids. At this point I probably should be deleting a few.

First off, let's start with the fun fact that for a quick run to the park, you need to pack like you're going camping in the Ozarks: sunscreen (there's nothing like showing up to the park, finding out it's ninety degrees in the shade, and realizing you forgot sunscreen), extra clothes (there's no such thing as a three-year-old who's 100 percent potty trained), water (because the closest working drinking fountain will probably be at your house), snacks, sand toys, Band-Aids, Purell, a blanket, and tranquilizer darts. Forget any one of these things and suddenly, you are Mooch Mom surrounded by Moms Who Clearly Have Their Shit Together More Than You Do. Hey, if I want to feel crappy about my parenting skills I can do that in the privacy of my own home!

But let's just say that by some miracle, you manage to bring enough stuff that you don't need to go home twenty minutes after you arrive. You're still not in for a good time. Let me break it down.

The Swings

Since my kids were little, all they've wanted to do is be on the swings. The entire time. And despite the fact that they are no longer babies and are currently in possession of working legs, they still want me to push them. *I don't want to push my kids on the swings anymore!* I have earned the right to sit on my ass and read Facebook on my phone. I mean, hello, isn't that why God made the Facebook app for iPhones? And what is it about a moving swing that makes it invisible to kids? I don't think I've ever gone to the park and not witnessed a kid get accidentally kicked in the face or knocked over by a high swinger. It makes it impossible to look away. Letting a small child walk near swings is like letting a drunk loose on a construction site. Do it at your own risk.

Public Restrooms

Even if you make your kids go to the bathroom before you leave, within seconds of arrival and then in ten-minute intervals moving forward, someone will have to pee. I don't know about you, but I've never seen a public park restroom that didn't require a hazmat suit to enter. And yeah, if you have boys you are probably laughing at me right now, but I tried to get my daughter to squat behind a tree and she ended up with wet shoes and some dirty stares from a couple groping each other on a blanket nearby. Which brings me to . . .

PDA

What's with the park porn? *Stop making out on blankets! No one wants to see that!* You wouldn't go to town in the middle of a movie theater showing a Pixar movie! This is the same thing! The next time I go to the park I'm going to bring a spray bottle and treat all fondling couples like naughty cats and squirt them in the face.

Ice Cream Truck

The ice cream man never fails to show up and remind me that I'm the worst kind of mom—the kind who forgets to bring cash. The ice-cream man is like an old-school drug pusher, except instead of meth, he deals Nutty Buddies. On second thought, that's a bit naïve. He probably sells plenty of meth.

Sand

It's everywhere and it's dirty. Even the ball pit at Chuck E. Cheese's gets cleaned every now and then; the sand at the park just collects germs from poop, cigarettes, animals, and other gross stuff year after year. And yet, what do kids do the second they arrive? Take their shoes off and make a beeline for the sandbox. It's disgusting. Of course even with their shoes off, somehow kids end up trekking it into the house, and you can't get it completely out of their hair or your carpet for weeks. I have an idea for park planners: how about instead of sand, we just lay carpeting? Hey, it's gross, but at least we can vacuum.

Play Structures

Why do all of those play structures have to be thirty feet high? Aren't they supposed to be for kids? My heart stops beating every time one of my kids stands at the top of one yelling for me to look at them. I am looking! And I'm scared you're going to fall! By the way, most kids scream, "Watch me!" about eighty trillion times an hour. There doesn't seem to be one physical accomplishment, from making it across one monkey bar rung to kicking sand two feet, that kids don't feel requires a cheering section. Hey, kids, you're on a play structure, not *America's Got Talent*. Take it down a notch. *Quick tip:* When kids yell, "Watch me, Mommy!" never physically walk over when a thumbs-up will do.

Child Molesters

Is it just me or does every mom attempt to play the "connect the dude by himself with the kid who belongs to him" game? I feel like Detective Olivia Benson from *Law & Order: SVU*, mentally establishing a perimeter in case there's trouble and giving side-eye to every potential perp. *Why is that guy sitting by himself for so long? Do I need to have him reported? Oh wait, he just pulled out a bag of Pirate's Booty. Never mind. Wait! Did that panel van just drive around the block twice?* You may think I'm being paranoid. It's called good parenting! Look into it!

Sand Toys

So you screwed the pooch and forgot to bring a single sand toy with you. And of course, another mom showed up with the entire beach aisle from Target. Now your kid is attempting to borrow a sifter and the other kid is throwing shade! What the hell? Don't even feel bad! If you had brought sand toys, your kid would have no interest in playing with them. He only wants them because they don't belong to him. But hey, look on the bright side: it's only sand toys and not someone's wife!

Other Mothers

What is with that mom at the park who completely has her shit together? You know the one I mean: she's surrounded by kids, some hers, some yours. Why? Because despite the fact that she has four kids of her own, she found the time to pack Tupperware containers full of freshly sliced strawberries and some sort of weird exotic yet healthy snack like baba ghanoush that your kid would sooner sign themselves up for summer school than eat at home, yet suddenly there's your little angel, stuffing her face like she hasn't eaten in weeks. Of course, Other Mother just smiles serenely and says, "Don't worry! I have so much! She sure seems hungry!" which makes you want to punch her . . . or take her home and make her your sister wife.

Getting Home

I have a park six blocks from my house, so almost every time we go I get sucked in to letting the kids ride their bikes there. Inevitably, on the way home, I end up having to carry one of their bikes because they are "just too tired." Once we get home they need a bath, and I need a chiropractor. But the strangest part is, it seems like I get some kind of park amnesia, because a few days later, I hear those five words from another mom, "Let's go to the park," and find myself saying, "Yeah, okay. Sounds good."

When will I learn?

Other Activities That Are Completely Overrated

THE BEACH

The beach is basically just the park, only with thirty times the hassle. There's the horrendous traffic, impossible parking, burning-hot sand, scary waves, aggressive seagulls, and mountains of gear required to "enjoy" yourselves for a few hours before gathering it all back up, heading home, and nursing a sunburn for four days. Seriously, the beach makes the park seem like a shiatsu massage.

FOURTH OF JULY

If you know of a place where you can watch fireworks and avoid getting trampled to death in a crowd, by all means go for it (and e-mail me the details). But big firework displays almost always seem to be accompanied by crowds that have begun drinking in midafternoon, and by the time it's dark enough for the fireworks to begin they aren't capable of tying their shoes, let alone keeping it together around young kids. Isn't it best to protect our children from this? Honorable mention goes to the douchebag hawking glow-in-the-dark light sabers/oversized glasses/bracelets/neck-laces, promptly tacking another fifty dollars onto my night. Eff you very much.

PARADES

I really don't get the appeal of parades. What's so interesting about watching a trailer decorated with flowers and packed with a couple of E-list celebrities drive down the street that we need to arrive four hours early to sit on a blanket, in the cold, on the curb? Oh, I know—nothing.

CAMPING

I refuse to do any activity that requires a full day of packing, loading coolers, and lugging crap to the car, and culminates in building my own housing for the night. "But you get to expose kids to nature and go for a hike and sleep under the stars," you might argue. I would argue right back that we can do all of those things without driving for hours. It's called the backyard. A world of mosquitoes, raccoon poop, and prickly leaves is waiting for us just beyond the screen door; I can just step outside and voilà! It's nature minus carsickness. If the kids want to sleep in the backyard, they can have at it! At least if they get hungry they can walk inside, as opposed to my having to build a fire and roast a turkey dog.

PUPPET SHOWS

I've taken my kids to quite a few puppet shows, and all I have to say about that is, we have movies now. Maybe puppet shows were really something to see before there was radio or television or theater or any other kind of entertainment options. The only exception to this is watching your kids put on a puppet show. On second thought, naw.

COLOR ME MINE

Nothing like taking your kids to paint a couple of pieces of cheap pottery and leaving the place down eighty-seven bucks plus a pair of paint-splattered jeans. I just can't understand for the life of me how a tiny kitty statue can cost eighteen bucks pre-paint. Not to mention when my kid's ten minutes in and decides "the kitty needs spots, but Mommy has to do it"—well, okay, maybe I grabbed the brush away from her, but she was really screwing it up (see "Kids' Art: They're Not All Picassos," page 65). But worse than that, how can anyone look you in the eye and tell you that besides the exorbitant price of the pottery, you need to pay an hourly fee to sit and paint it? I asked about this once and I was told that they had to charge for the supplies that are used. Come on! What kind of a business model is this? When I go get my hair cut, I pay for the haircut; I don't get charged an hourly "scissors toll" and a "comb usage fee" on top of that. And, hey, hairdressers, don't get any ideas. Bottom line: this is a waste of money.

Sisterhood of the Traveling Spanx

O nce you have kids, one of the first things to take a major hit is your old *Sex and the City*–type social life. Yes, *I know, I know,* you have really amazing friends and nothing, especially not the mere act of becoming a mom, will change that! Your friendships are different! They are deep and meaningful, built on formative life experiences and maintained by long daily phoners and weekly mimosa brunches. Uh-huh.

Think about it: when is the last time you talked to the "Samantha" of your old group? Was it when she had her thirty-fifth birthday party at that authentic karaoke bar in a sort of sketchy part of town? You'd had a baby three weeks before but you tried to muscle through to prove that *you're not going to be one of those moms who bails on all her besties just because you had a baby.* But you still ended up leaving after half an hour because your breasts were leaking and you couldn't stop crying.

Or what about the last time you saw the "Miranda" (not that anyone ever admits to being the Miranda, so chances are she doesn't know she's the Miranda)? Was it when she accidentally got pregnant by her married boss and was trying to figure out whether or not to keep the baby because, after all, she's thirty-six and this might be her one and only chance to become a mother? No, wait, you only talked to her on the phone about it, because the kids were on winter break and you couldn't find a sitter. Anyway, that was like eight months ago. Shit, you totally need to call and see how that all turned out.

And how about the "Charlotte"? Trick question—there is no Charlotte; that was an unrealistic character. And I would ask you about the "Carrie," but you are the Carrie, right? Everyone thinks they're the Carrie.

The point is, if you are honest with yourself, you will see that your life has changed and, like every other woman whose social life has been devastated by children, you've found it necessary to find new friends who are going through what you're going through. You've been forced to build a new social tapestry of all different sorts of moms, and chances are not one of them resembles a hip character from a zeitgeisty sitcom. In fact, I'll bet one of them has even been known to wear chinos and Crocs.

When I first had a baby I needed friends, and I collected them in all sorts of places: Target, Mommy and Me, and the pediatrician's office were all hotbeds of anxious new-mom activity, and I took full advantage of all of these new-friend-making ops. I arranged more hookups than Charlie Sheen at the AVN Awards. And, thankfully, many of the women I met during that time of my life are still my friends. New moms are like soldiers in a foxhole: we meet each other at our most scared and vulnerable, and learn to rely on each other, to help each other out in an emergency, and to show up and have each other's backs even if we suspect one of us may be out of her fucking mind. Mom Code!

I met my friend Lara at a Mommy and Me when our babies were just six months old (if you're wondering how someone like me could go to Mommy and Me you can read all about it in *Sippy Cups Are Not for Chardonnay*). She seemed a lot less gung ho than most of the other first-timers in the group, which is a quality I'm attracted to in a person. We bonded over a mutual distaste for puppet shows and songs involving blackbirds. Then during the Q & A, I asked the instructor how soon I was going to regain my will to live and Lara smiled at me. I was thrilled to finally feel a connection with someone not wearing a diaper, so I worked up my courage and casually asked her if she wanted to exchange information.

The first time we hung out together, we took our infants to a park and went for a walk, stopping every ninety seconds to readjust them in their strollers or to stick a pacifier back in one of their mouths, or to just lean over them and make sure they were still breathing. We talked about our old lives a little bit and determined that we had enough in common to warrant a second date! After determining that neither of us had anything beyond that Mommy and Me class so much as penciled into our day planners for the next decade, we made plans to get together the very next day.

The following morning I had a huge fight with my husband. It was the kind of fight I only had with him in the very beginning of our relationship, before I fully trusted him; in the first year after we had a baby; and any time I'd downed thirteen wine coolers. We could've been fighting about anything. I was paranoid, ragey, and constantly thinking that he was going to leave me. So in my postpartum freak-out I yelled something to him along the lines of, "Well if I'm so horrible, maybe we should just get a divorce!"

And that's when my new-mom friend Lara pulled up in her Honda Pilot.

It took her a while to get to the front door since she had to unfold her stroller, figure out how to transfer her sleeping infant out of the car without waking her, attempt to wedge her humongous and overpacked diaper bag into the too-small basket underneath the stroller (note to Graco: new moms pack to go to the park for a few hours like we're going on a monthlong polar excursion to Antarctica, so we're gonna need bigger baskets), and then finally amble up my walk. But it still didn't buy me enough time to get my shit together.

I answered the door looking like I'd just watched the director's cut of *Schindler's List* and let Lara know that I needed a minute. She took one look at my teary face and just said, "No worries. Just come out when you're ready."

I didn't want to leave things unresolved, but my husband refused to continue arguing with me while someone was waiting outside and said we'd have to talk later. My husband's actually never been one to adhere to rules like "never go to bed angry"; in fact, my being upset is like Ambien to him. He's famous for falling asleep right smack in the middle of an argument just when I'm about to really bring home a great point about why he's wrong.

I left feeling completely unsettled and panicky (not unlike how I felt 98 percent of the time during the first year of parenting), and spent the entire walk with my new friend crying and obsessing about the big fight. I admitted to her how I'd dropped the D bomb and that I was worried my husband was sick of me, my moods, and my crappy attitude. I wondered if I was a horrible wife and mother. Basically I told her what a complete mess I felt like. I knew I must've sounded like a complete lunatic but I couldn't stop myself. I was pretty sure I'd ruined my chances with her and I wouldn't have been surprised if she never called again.

But she did call again and never mentioned what a mental case I'd been. In fact, she became one of my closest friends.

Years later I asked her what was going through her head that day and if she'd thought I was crazy. "No," she said. "I felt relieved because I thought I was the only one who was going through that. It made me like you even more." Bam. Instant war buddies.

The new-mommy friends are important, but as our kids get older making friends becomes more complicated: First off, to hang out with another mom, our kids need to be about the same age and probably into the same sport or activity; our kids have to like each other, and if there are siblings, the siblings have to get along with the other kids; if we have spouses, they have to get along, or at least not hate each other; and our spouse needs to like our new-mom friend but *not too much* or the whole relationship won't work. Our social connections become more complex than the plot of *Inception*.

Even if it all lines up, we still need to be picky. With so little time to spare, we need friends who get it and get us. Personally, with three kids to deal with, I need friends who understand my limitations and have lowered their expectations. They get that although I said I'd be willing to go to an art opening on Saturday night, by the time the weekend rolls around I can only muster up enough energy to watch *The Voice* and eat a bowl of cereal. I need friends who understand that my version of dressing up is putting on special-occasion flip-flops. Yeah, bitch, they're sparkly and fabulous, yet they can be worn to wash the car!

But where do we make friends like this?

Parenting fact: you need a bestie. Parenting problem: making friends hasn't gotten easier since we were in high school. And nowadays we need to have a little more in common to form a truly lasting connection. Instead of bonding over a pregnancy scare, you may be bonding over your fourth failed round of IVF. Instead of nursing your friend through her parents' divorce, she might be nursing you through your divorce. But how can you tell if a mom has the makings of a BFF just from seeing her at Tiny Feet Soccer once a week?

Wouldn't it be great if there was a way to weed out the boring moms, the Judge Judys, and the meanies and find your perfect match: a mom with kids the same age as yours, a wicked yet kind sense of humor, and a love of reality TV? I only wish there were dating profiles for making mommy friends. Think what a time saver that would be! Seriously, someone should create that and kick me about 15 percent equity for the concept! Someone who doesn't have kids so they have more time and energy on their hands for starting small businesses, or cooking pancakes from scratch, or learning to use their Keurig. (What? It's a long manual.) All right, I'm going to write myself an ad and someone go ahead and develop the app; I'll be waiting.

DESPERATELY SEEKING:
NEW SIDEKICK/WILLING WINGWOMAN/
ALL-AROUND BESTIE

Smart-ass, married mom of three sporadically charming girls seeking funny friends with kids approximately the same ages for long, lazy afternoons at Chuck E. Cheese's, rehashing *Real Housewives,* and commiserating about the exhausting and unrelenting nature of parenting. I'm interested in a long-term commitment. The right person could possibly be used as an emergency contact on school forms.

About me: I'm forty-one years old (but with the energy of someone much much older), I hate quinoa, I love Katy Perry, and I often forget my reusable bags at the grocery store. I used to enjoy travel but I don't do it much anymore because my kids get carsick. (True story: one of my girls puked on a five-minute drive to the mall—although that could've been attributed to some questionable grocery-store sushi she ate earlier in the day . . . look, we may never know for sure, but the point is, if travel is a big thing for you, this may be a deal breaker.) I do enjoy trips to museums and exhibits, but I'm warning you that I'm not the type to bring a picnic lunch to eat on the front lawn. I'm way more likely to say, "Screw it," and buy overpriced sandwiches from the café.

In my free time I enjoy reading *Us Weekly* and going swimming in other people's pools. Do you have a pool? Oh, dear God, please have a pool.

How would I describe my parenting style? I would describe my parenting style as fairly laid-back with a small-to-large dose of neurotic. I'm not going to make my kids wash their hands thirty times a day, but I have been known to scream, *"Hold hands!"* five times in a parking lot. I don't keep soda in the house but I'm fine if they want to order it in a restaurant. Just an aside, I hope you're not one of those moms who forces their kids to drink water in a restaurant while my kids drink Sprite or lemonade right in front of them. Because come on, let them live a little! (If my just saying "live a little" rubbed you the wrong way, we are probably not a match.)

What is my discipline style? I do discipline my kids when it's necessary but I'm not a yeller . . . if there are witnesses.

Five things I couldn't live without: My microwave, drive-throughs, *The Real Housewives of Beverly Hills*, *The Real Housewives of Orange County*, *The Real Housewives of New York*, *48 Hours* mysteries, *20/20*. Oh, and baby wipes: those suckers handle 90 percent of the cleaning I attempt.

Turn-ons: Chuck E. Cheese's coupons, extremely easy Crock-Pot recipes, disposable diapers, the words "Put your money away! This is my treat!" Friends who will let me slide on claiming to be forty-one. Also people who have swimming pools.

Turnoffs: Convenience stores that won't let my kids use their bathrooms, parenting experts, petting zoos, lactivists, mall Santas, Color Me Mine, *Caillou.*

What my friends say is my best quality: Um, okay, well, I e-mailed them repeatedly about this and they haven't gotten back to me on it *yet* but as soon as they do I will add it to my profile.

You: Are you still reading? If so, maybe you're my person. Please be laid-back, noncompetitive, and not too into crafts. Having grown up in the seventies is a plus. I'm looking for a fun mom who tries not to give her kids too much sugar but isn't above sneaking into their stash of Halloween candy and eating it herself. I'm looking for that special friend I can text if I'm running late for pickup and just say, "Can you grab my kids?" and I'll know when I get to them that they will be safe, happy, and probably wearing sunscreen. I like a mom who has an extra booster seat in her car, just in case.

It would be cool if your favorite Real Housewife is Heather from *RHONY.* Holla!

I like someone who always has a good, and more importantly a survivable, idea for what we can do for the Fourth of July. I'm looking for friends who get it. If my kid has a massive meltdown because we were at the beach and the sand felt too hot and the lifeguard blew his whistle too loud, I want a mom who says to me, "What the fuck was up with that lifeguard and his fucking whistle?" and then turns to my kid and says, "Let's find your flip-flops," not a mom who rolls her eyes and wonders aloud if my kid might have sensory integration disorder.

I like a mom who doesn't give a shit if I miss her birthday because, come on, we're adults. Oh, and you must own a television. Did I mention I would love it if you had a pool?

If you fit this bill, then come on over and have a rest on my couch—I'll even give it a quick once-over with some wipes. We'll watch some *Real Housewives* and I'll make you a cup of coffee. That is, if I can sort out this effing Keurig. Maybe you can help?

So let's say through your kids' lives you've managed to pull off meeting a few fun moms and now you have a real circle of friends. Or at least a semicircle. Okay, a curve. The point is, you have a friend. Now you can just sit back and coast until retirement, when you can hang out in the common room at the assisted living home bragging about your grandkids and cheating at bingo, right? Not so fast. Women's friendships aren't like men's. Women's friendships require upkeep.

Men crack me up because a man can make a friend in junior high, see him all of four times since then, and still consider him one of his closest buddies thirty years later. I've been married to my husband for ten years and I still sometimes hear about a "good friend" of his I've never ever heard mentioned before. A man can also consider another man a "good friend" when he doesn't even know the most basic information about the guy. Ask him when his friend's birthday is, if his friend is planning to have kids, if he's happy in his marriage, and he'll say, "I don't know. It never came up. We mostly talk about cars." Seriously, there are men who can consider another guy a friend without even knowing his name. That's why so many guys call each other bro.

Female friendships are much more delicate than the male variety. Women are high maintenance. If friendship were like the military, women would have to remain on active duty while men could stay in the reserves, sometimes never once getting called to battle. Very little is expected of men in their friendships, but women want you to return phone calls and texts, like *that day*, and to actually get together every so often—I know, tedious, right? Which is why the best mom friends are geographically convenient. A next-door neighbor is ideal.

But it is nearly inevitable that the second you become extremely close friends with someone who lives nearby and with whom you have plenty in common, they will suddenly decide to completely change their lives and move to Montana. "We've always wanted to live in Big Sky Country! We're going to build our own house and let the laundry air-dry on the line outside. We won't even have to have jobs because it's so inexpensive to live there that we'll be able to survive strictly on our new Etsy store! I think we're just looking for a slower pace and Montana is such a beautiful place to raise kids. Plus, I've always wanted little Claire to know the joy of her own pet alpaca. You guys should totally do it too!"

You will feel betrayed and be sad. But don't go crazy and follow them to Montana, no matter how bad the school system sucks where you are and no matter how amazing your friend's new converted farmhouse looks in all the photos. Look, I don't care that they got twenty-five hundred square feet on two acres for two hundred grand. And I don't care that they are "unschooling" their kids and raising freethinkers in nature who are thriving and happy. Just grieve the loss and move on. Anyway, they'll be back. They always come back. They'll miss the smog.

Sure, it sucks, but it's not impossible to remain friends. That's why God invented Facebook. Seriously, if it wasn't for Facebook, I'd probably only have about four friends total. And if you're one of those people who's like, "I'm just really not into Facebook. I prefer to spend time with my kids and enjoy authentic experiences," well, maybe you just don't want to have friends.

Sometimes, even if your friend doesn't move away, mom friendships may not last. First off, life changes quickly as a parent. Maybe you saw each other every day while the kids were in preschool, but when they started at different elementary schools your schedules just didn't mesh anymore. Or maybe one of you went on to have six more kids and the other one found that to be completely Kate Gosselin–level crazy. Or maybe you stayed friends for years while the kids were friends, but when the kids grew apart, you realized that you had nothing really to talk about. It's okay. Let her go. You had a good run. But next time maybe opt for friendship bracelets over those matching BFF tattoos that seemed so perfect on your girls' trip to Mazatlán.

Friend Deal Breakers

Just like with dating, when it comes to making friends, there are going to be qualities that you find to be a major turnoff. You may spot these problems right away or a little too late, but either way, sometimes you just know it's not going to work out. I asked my Facebook friends to tell me their mom-friend deal breakers and then had a good laugh at the responses:

> One of my friends from school has a daughter named Jocelyn. The mom likes to pass out business cards that say "Jocelyn's Mom" with her contact info on them for playdates. I think it's super weird.

> Dieting, fasting, weight-obsessed moms. I have girls, we eat cake.

> Scrapbooking moms.

> Ones who act like the mean girls in high school. "Mean Women." Is there a movie about that? Because there should be.

> The one who disciplines your kid right in front of you, talks about how much her husband makes, and constantly talks about how advanced her kid is. And no I don't believe for a second that her baby spoke at six months.

Gun owners. If my kid is going to be playing at their house, I don't need that extra worry.

Religious fanatics.

The ones who bring their husbands to every play-date, outing, or kids' party. What is up with that??

The mom whose child you've picked up after school and had playdates with at your house for a year and has never returned the favor.

The ones who make those lunch box art-project meals. Like seriously?

Moms who are selling something constantly, e.g., Avon, Pampered Chef, candles, natural healing oils.

I had a mom friend tell me she didn't believe in evolution. Evolution is my deal breaker.

Well my ex–best friend sexted my husband, so yeah, that was a deal breaker . . .

One mom I was friends with served breast milk cookies! I'm out.

I had someone stop talking to me for a bit because my daughter won a school election. She told me she "just needed some time."

American Girl vs. Barbie

M y youngest kid has a shit-ton of Barbie dolls and I don't have an issue with it. Seriously though, Barbie and her band of spin-offs have pretty much taken over the house. They have overflowed the toy room's colorful fabric boxes and filled extra bins in the bedroom, and when they needed more room they began setting up alternative housing in her closet.

It's like a mini Barbie micro-city in my house. There are Barbie cars, a Barbie pool—conveniently there is also a Barbie lifeguard stand, which was bought separately, and of course the requisite number of bikini-clad Barbies to hang around the pool, although they all seem to lose their bathing suits in record time. There's a Barbie dentist, a Barbie dentist's chair with dental hygienist Barbie, and at one point we even had a Barbie plane so she could fly around with her fashionista friends. The only thing we don't have is the Barbie camper, because seriously, when is the last time you saw a tall blonde in loads of makeup and six-inch heels who had any interest in camping? Except maybe at Burning Man.

Since the Barbies obviously outnumber family members, my only concern is that they may start petitioning for more rights in the house. Maybe they'll form a little Barbie government with Barbie bylaws, like no one can leave the house without being properly accessorized or everyone must wear pink at all times. It's possible that the Barbies have already been doing this and are very strict, because I've come across a few headless ones lately. I wouldn't be at all shocked to find out there is a Barbie dictator in our midst.

I know a lot of parents have a hate-on for Barbie, what with her unrealistic proportions and her obsession with pink cars and metrosexual boyfriends. Moms have concerns, like why are they all so anorexic? Why do they dress like hos? Why are there so few Barbies of color? These are all good questions and I don't have good answers to them, but I'll tell you what the answer isn't: those snotty bitches from the higher tax bracket otherwise known as American Girl dolls.

For the price of one American Girl doll, I can buy like fifteen Barbies. And I have.

Even though I have three girls, I had no idea American Girl dolls even existed until my oldest daughter started asking for one because all her friends each had one. Correction: all her friends had several. So I went over to the American Girl website and when I got a look at the price tags, my look of surprise almost broke straight through my Botox. These dolls start at over a hundred bucks! And that's just for the doll. The clothes are insanely overpriced—you're going to spend at least thirty dollars for a simple dress (shoes and bag not included)—and there ain't no T.J.Maxx for an American Girl doll's clothes.

The whole thing is quite the racket: you can only buy American Girl dolls from their website or from the American Girl doll store, conveniently located in just thirteen cities in the entire United States. If you are (un)lucky enough to live in close enough proximity to one of these stores, your daughter can take her doll out to lunch there! But you may want to go ahead and mortgage your home before you even get in the car. *Lunch is $23 per person, excluding tax and gratuity. Afternoon Tea is $20 per person, excluding tax and gratuity, and dinner is $24 per person, excluding tax and gratuity.* Twenty dollars for fucking tea! Are you shitting me? Are these fucking dolls sitting down with the queen? In what alternate universe are regular folk taking their dolls out to have a cucumber sandwich and twenty-dollar tea? By the way, your doll doesn't actually drink tea! She's not fucking alive! Hang on, I need to go calm down a minute. Okay, I'm back.

Guess what else you can do with your doll if you have eighty thousand dollars lying around? You can take your American Girl doll to the American Girl doll hospital. Yes, if your doll's leg falls off or if her eye pops out, you can ship her off to the hospital. I checked into the prices for this service, and let's just say you'd probably get a smaller bill if you took yourself to the ER. I know someone who had to take Molly, the World War II supporter, to the American Girl doll hospital when her braids came out. It cost $100 to "fix"! And—typical—the American Girl doll hospital doesn't accept Blue Cross.

Many moms have this notion that American Girl dolls are superior to Barbie because American Girl dolls are more wholesome. I've heard people say, "American Girl dolls are about being friends with other girls and caring about other people. Barbies are just about being pretty and popular and caring only about yourself." It's true that American Girl offers a variety of historical dolls, like Addy Walker, a

Civil War–era doll who, along with her mother, has escaped slavery. She's looking to find her father and brother who've been sold away. Awesome! Who wants tea? There's also Kaya, an American Indian doll who comes with a pow-wow dress and a tepee (and by "comes with," I mean you can buy them for $186 total).

I'm sure the historic dolls are meant to set a nice example. I mean, I get it, Kaya, it's tough to be superficial when you have to hunt for salmon and buffalo to survive. But I've never met a single kid who owned an Addy or a Kaya. Even Josefina, our "hopeful New Mexican girl" from the 1820s, usually gets the shaft. And that's because they aren't the popular girls.

I have, however, met a bunch of girls who have McKenna! She's blond! She lurves gymnastics! Or how about one of the latest "it" dolls, Isabelle? Isabelle's studying ballet at a performing arts school! And she has a flair for designing ballet costumes, because of course she does.

I know what you're going to say: "But Barbie dresses so slutty! At least American Girl dolls are actually girls and not boobalicious women like Barbie."

Yes, you're right. I can't really defend Barbie. In fact, I just did a little Googling and found a link to Barbie in a catsuit wearing Christian Louboutins. Okay, that's why we should just be happy that at least Barbie's an adult, right? An adult who can make her own decisions on what to spend her cash on—be it breast-enhancement surgery or Loubs!

Look, it's all a little depressing, but I've decided not to make myself too crazy about it. I had Barbie dolls as a kid and I don't believe I have to look like a Barbie doll to be a worthy person or to be loved. I just liked putting their outfits on and off and trying to make their knees hyper-extend. I also need to look on the bright side: the other day my kid insisted on purchasing an entire Barbie wedding set with her own allowance money that she'd saved up. It was a box containing a groom, bride, maid of honor, and flower girl—plus a cake and some gifts (the entire set came to less than $30—suck on that, American Girl!). I had no idea why she wanted this wedding collection so much. She certainly didn't get it from me! My husband and I had the most low-key wedding ever and never make our kids look at pictures, and I've only rarely attempted to model my wedding dress and cried because I couldn't zip it up anymore. But here's the cool thing: my kids played wedding with the dolls non-stop, but the ones who were getting married were . . . bride Barbie and maid–of–honor Barbie. And that was no accident. It was explained to me that "ladies can marry ladies and men can marry men." That's right, friends, my little

Barbie lovers are all for equal rights, and so with values intact, they have my blessing to play with whatever dolls they want. Even if they do wear Louboutins and a tube top. Would that open-minded shit fly in Kaya's tepee or Josefina's *rancho*? No, I don't think so.

The Hunger Games:
Lunch Box Edition

— - - — — - - — — —

Since when did making your kids' lunch become an opportunity for one-upmanship? Have you ever prepared your child a whole wheat tortilla roll-up with hand-shaved carrots, thinly sliced cucumber, organic turkey, and hummus? Well, stop it. You're making the rest of us look bad. And if you don't believe me that this lunch thing has gotten out of control, go to Pinterest and type in "ideas for kids' lunches." But be prepared to immediately give your children up for adoption to better families—families with their very own Pinterest sites devoted to kids, food, and fun!

I'm sorry, but there's just no way you can come up with creative shit to put in your kids' lunches every single day, especially when you have more than one kid. I can barely figure out what I'm going to eat, let alone what three picky eaters will get excited about.

Don't get me wrong; I've attempted creativity in the past. There was a time when my kids were younger and I was newer to the parenting game when I gave it a try. Something caught my eye in a magazine about taking a cookie cutter and using it to make sandwiches come out in cute shapes like a star or a dinosaur or a ghost. It seemed like a perfect way to add a little bit of *Martha Stewart Living* into my Roseanne Conner existence. *Why not?* I thought to myself. *It will be fun!* I figured, hey, I'm not usually known for my sandwich whimsy, so this will really surprise them. In practice, however, it sucked.

First off, the fact that I didn't own any cookie cutters should have been a tip-off that I was being overambitious. At this point in my life I'm too lazy to even buy the tube of cookie dough you have to slice. When the R & D department of Toll House came out with the kind that is *pre-sliced* into little cookie-sized dough patties, I was the consumer they had in mind. But I went ahead on my fool's mission. When I cut a star into my first sandwich, I realized that I had a far more serious problem than supplies. The star was too small. One star was not big enough to eat alone as the main part of the lunch. Not by a long shot. I was going to need at least three stars.

But there was no way to get more than one star out of one sandwich, because after punching out the star what you were left with, sandwich-wise, was mostly crust. So, unless Sara Lee invented bigger bread slices, I was going to need more than one sandwich per kid. When you multiply four bread slices by three children, we're talking a loaf of bread per lunch. Sorry, I'm not Donald Trump.

It just seems like it was never this difficult when we were kids. Back then your mom would throw a tuna sandwich with mayo and a Hostess cupcake into a brown paper bag or a Bionic Woman metal lunch box and call it a day. Not that this was necessarily a good thing: room-temp tuna doesn't travel well, so by noon all the kids in class would be gagging on fumes. And by the time you took your tuna out it would have formed into a giant ball of coagulated tuna and soggy bread, which would then promptly get thrown in the trash. As if that weren't bad enough, my mom took it a step further and went for sardines, egg salad, and even liverwurst. It's a wonder I ever weighed more than seventy-eight pounds. I'm not bitter though. I mean, sure I got teased a lot by the other kids and no one ever wanted to sit next to me at lunch, but it built character and made me a stronger person. At least that's what my therapist tells me when I see her twice a week.

But nowadays we're all about health. Everyone's a food-safety Nazi ever since some studies came out to tell us that if our kid's lunch dips below forty degrees, bacteria are going to spread around faster than Jennifer Aniston pregnancy rumors. Oh, yeah, lunch box cooling systems are big business now. Target has an entire aisle devoted to Spider-Man gel packs and plastic ices shaped like ladybugs, not to mention insulated sacks so high-tech they look like something astronauts take out into space to chill their Tang. Yet, despite all this, according to studies 90 percent of lunches packed with even the most expensive ice packs still are at unhealthy temperatures once they have been sitting for two hours. But come on, did we really think that a little gel pack would make our kids feel like they're eating lunch in Alaska? No. We do it because it makes us feel like we're trying.

As I've stated time and time again (many times in this book), I'm not against trying to get my kids to eat healthy. In fact, I pack something healthy in my kids' lunches every day. I know they're probably not going to eat it, but I still continue the charade. Let's be honest, we all throw something in our kid's lunch that's just for show. I once packed the same green apple in my older daughter's lunch five days straight; every day it went to school, every day it came back home. After the first few days without even a bite being taken out, it became a standoff—a battle of wills waged via bruised produce. I'd lovingly prepare a brand-new turkey sandwich, add in a couple of cookies, and tuck that same damn apple back in behind a napkin. By Friday, I finally had to throw the apple away before it began to resemble a Furby. I almost let her think she'd won, but at the last second I snuck in some snap peas. I don't go down without a fight.

If I'm being honest, the apples I pack are probably more for me. I make sure there's something healthy in there in case I have an audience. I don't want a busybody mom lunch-table volunteer judging me for packing a lunch made up solely of nitrate-free salami and a couple of Nutter Butters, despite the fact that that's what she'll probably eat.

Even if your kids are naturally healthy eaters, you really can't win. My twins love broccoli soup that I lovingly prepare in my Cuisinart from fresh organic broccoli picked up at my local farmer's market. Either that, or it's take-out soup from California Chicken Cafe. For a while I would make a special trip to get that broccoli soup because, ZOMG! My Kids Are Eating Broccoli Soup! I would pack the soup into thermoses and add a few Ritz crackers and feel amazing about my parenting for the rest of the day—praying that some other parent would catch sight of my kids inhaling pureed broccoli and immediately write up a story about me for the school newspaper. But then my kids started to complain because they said the other kids were making fun of them because their soup looked weird and smelled bad. Yeah, apparently I'm ruining my kids' lunch-table cred by packing smelly green soup.

And I do understand how they feel—boy, do I ever! I feel for my little gals being shunned at the lunch table for their stinky soup. But you know what? I'm going to keep on giving them that broccoli soup. That broccoli soup is building character. It's going to make them stronger people with excellent core values! At least that's what I hope they'll hear when I'm paying for all their future therapy.

Bedtime: The Widow Maker

s a rule, for most parents, our kids' bedtime is by far our favorite part of the day. Unfortunately, for kids, bedtime is by far their worst part of the day. But I'm getting ahead of myself. In the beginning, before there's bedtime, there's just getting the baby to sleep.

There's a reason that as soon as we have a baby we become obsessed with getting them to sleep, so we can sleep. It's because sleep deprivation is the devil and one of the true drawbacks of bringing human life into this world. Hello! Sleep deprivation is an approved method of torture! Our own government uses it to get enemies to give up information. Surely a couple of vulnerable new parents are no match for sleep deprivation's brutality. So it's no wonder that most new parents' bookshelves are lined with titles such as *The No-Cry Sleep Solution* and *Solve Your Child's Sleep Problems*. There are literally entire schools of thought on how to get babies to go the f**k to sleep (not to mention that *Go the F**k to Sleep* itself was a runaway bestseller). Naturally, a lot of it is contradictory. For instance: According to Ferber, the American Academy of Pediatrics, and Brazelton, whatever you do, you shouldn't bring the baby into your bed for fear of creating a controlling monster, if not a future dictator. But according to Dr. Sears, if your baby is having trouble going back to sleep, consider . . . you guessed it: putting him in your bed. Hope you like uniforms and military parades.

You gotta wonder what parents did before there was sleep training and sleep whisperers and a million techniques that promise a simple solution to get your baby to go to sleep. Although it was probably easier back when cribs were pimped out with more plush shit than Beyoncé's dressing room. They could toss in down comforters, blankets, pillows, and stuffed animals. Plus, babies were encouraged to curl up like little potato bugs and sleep on their stomachs. Nowadays we're all about Back to Sleep and crib safety. In our parents' day, crib safety meant trying not to ash your Pall Mall into the bassinet. But now, forget about those teddy bears, and if you have crib bumpers people will look at you like you just gave your baby a tattoo.

Like every other new parent, I could barely function the first couple of months of my daughter's life, and I was desperate for her to sleep (you can read all about it in *Sippy Cups Are Not for Chardonnay*—not to worry if you need to go purchase a copy, I'll wait). So the first time my oldest daughter slept from nine thirty p.m. to six thirty a.m. it was like the sky clearing after a thunderstorm. Cue the angels' choir! Mentally I felt jaunty, like I should be wearing a little chauffeur's cap and riding pants or maybe sitting by a lake skipping rocks while whistling an old-timey tune, shouting out to people, "I'm a brand-new gal, I tell ya!" It's amazing what sleep will do for your overall outlook. And antidepressants—let's not discount those delightful little pharmaceutical life preservers that some of us need to get through the hormonal early months. The point is, no matter what your experience is with a newborn, when that kid sleeps straight through the night, you will feel like you won parenting.

And it *will* be great—for a while. You might even get cocky, thinking, *What are all these new moms complaining about? My baby sleeps like it's her job! And all I had to do was X, Y, or Z!* But slow down, missy. It's probably nothing you did. Babies mostly start sleeping through the night due to a combination of genetics and their own circadian rhythms, not because you had the stroke of genius to buy a stuffed lamb that has the sound of a human heartbeat in it. Whether your kid starts sleeping well at three weeks, three months, or a year, the downside is that it gives you a false sense of security that you've got this, that from here on out it's going to be smooth sailing.

But just know that at some point in the near future, the sleep issue will again drop your entire existence in a blender and push puree. Parenthood is fickle that way.

Even if your kid is a champion sleeper, when they hit the toddler stage, they will no longer take bedtime lying down. And there's a reason for that: Kids all have an acute case of #FOMO (that's "fear of missing out" if you're #Over35). Kids imagine that the second they fall asleep some sort of party bus is going to roll up full of preschoolers, cotton candy, puppies, and magicians. Who the hell would want to sleep through that? Personally, I kind of get where kids are coming from: I've never been able to leave a club without worrying that no matter how late it is, ten minutes after I'm gone Prince is going to show up and play a free show with three hours of new material off of his never-to-be-released album. Stop laughing. I go to clubs once every . . . presidential election or so.

Of course, even if we understand where kids are coming from, we still need them to go to bed; *we live for them to go to bed!* It's our time, damn it! So when a wrench is thrown into your plans, you may find yourself consulting an expert or two. Most articles about toddlers and sleep stress a consistent bedtime routine: bath, stories, kisses, good night. And that can definitely help. But even if you start bath time early, read every Pigeon book Mo Willems ever wrote, give endless kisses, deliver them a little warm milk, and say "sweet dreams," the second you hightail it out to the couch to catch up on *Scandal* you may well find yourself getting called back into your kid's room—for the next three hours.

This is where the experts suggest trying to anticipate every single one of your child's various—and, might I add, unreasonable—needs before you tuck them in. Just be careful with that because you may accidentally back yourself into a corner. When my sister-in-law was pregnant with her second child she realized that her three-year-old son's bedtime routine had slowly ballooned into a two-hour affair consisting of four stories, multiple monster checks, late night snacks, extra cuddles, specific arrangement of stuffed animals, etc. She knew she wouldn't be able to keep that up once the baby was born. But she was petrified that her kid wouldn't go to bed without it. And she was right. She tried to trim it back after her new daughter arrived, but eventually she had to admit defeat and just let him stay up and watch *Shark Tank*.

Some kids go through a period where they just *don't sleep*. One of my twins went through this chilling phase when she was about two. She had no interest in sleeping and no tolerance for the mere suggestion of sleeping, and was also disgusted that anyone else in our house would want to do anything so distasteful and bourgeois as putting their head on a pillow and lying still for a few hours. "Don't sleep, Mommy!" she'd scream at me if I dared rest my head on the couch cushion—while sitting up. I didn't have the balls to actually lie down on the couch in front of her.

One night while she was in this phase I nearly lost it completely. I knew it was going to be bad because she'd had a horrible attitude just getting ready for bed. First she demanded milk, and not in a pink sippy cup, in an *orange* one! Then the crib was lowered on one side so that she could climb in because she *needs to do it herself*! Then she spilled some milk on her jammies so she required *new ones now*! And then the lights were lowered—but not too low, because *that's too dark*—and music was turned on but *not*

James Taylor! And then finally I got a "night night, Mama." The door was quietly closed behind me but *not all the way!* And I tiptoed down the hall like a cat burglar. No sooner had I gotten to the living room than the screaming started. Bloodcurdling, make-you-want-to-slice-your-ears-off-with-a-paring-knife screaming. Nothing was wrong with her. How did I know this? Because she was yelling, "*I don't wanna go to bed!*" over and over between screams. I figured out the hard way that Internet advice isn't quite so helpful when it comes to this more extreme behavior. The popular advice is to be calm but firm, stand your ground even if your child whines or pleads, and don't engage in a power struggle. Apparently if you give in, you're just giving them the message that you can be swayed.

So we tried to be firm.

But she didn't make it easy. She just kept screaming while we sat in tense silence trying to pinpoint the exact moment our lives had gone off the rails. My husband self-medicated with vodka and I searched futilely for solace in game after game of Brick Breaker (a strong precursor to Candy Crush) on my BlackBerry. Every so often we wondered how long it could go on. Would she be able to scream all night? Would her twin sister sleep through it? Did behavior disorders have to be disclosed in private adoptions? Maybe, we thought, we could give her to the Duggars; I was sure they wouldn't even notice. We knew we had to establish boundaries with her, but we also wondered how we could do that without having to completely drop out of society, rent a bus, and go find a cabin somewhere so that our child could eat berries from the forest floor and scream to her heart's content. Maybe in the woods people would think we were just part of some sort of "let your inner wild child out"–type religion or that she was a witch.

But finally, she stopped screaming, and we realized our patience had paid off!

I'm fucking with you; she continued yelling for over two hours until she broke us completely and we were forced to go in and get her. Of course the second we walked in, she gave us a huge smile as if she'd just been treating us to a guided meditation for the past two hours and not making us question our decision to have more kids.

I'd love to tell you that this one night was an isolated incident, but I think it was a tough couple of weeks . . . or years. It's all a blur. Let's not get stuck on the minor details. Admittedly this was pretty extreme and not everyone will have it so bad. But I know we're not alone either: I have friends who have told me tales of their toddlers shrieking like chimps, hurling everything out of their cribs, stripping themselves naked, and even taking off their diapers and throwing their poop around the room. Horrible, right? Really the only difference between toddlers and chimpanzees is that it's illegal to shoot your toddler with a tranquilizer dart in every state but Texas. (By the way, if you Googled that, I'm going to laugh so hard!)

Speaking of chimps, some toddlers figure out how to climb out of their cribs as early as a year or year and a half. When this happens, a lot of parents will erroneously assume that their simian prodigy must be ready for a big bed. Big mistake. Most toddlers are pretty decent about going to sleep as long as they feel safe in the maximum-security cell of crib bars and bumpers. But once they get a taste of the Big Bed, just like poor Brooks in *The Shawshank Redemption*, they're totally unable to deal with all that sweet freedom. Most of them will become confused and just get out of their bed and wander into the living room *every five seconds*, forcing you to spend the only free minutes of your evening walking them back in. Others will leave their bed and play with their toys all night. In the morning you'll innocently walk into their room and it will look like the place has been ransacked, only in this case the perp is in Little Mermaid footies and out cold in the middle of the crime scene. I'd say a better idea than jumping to the Big Bed too early is to get one of those crib nets. By the way, I've heard that crib nets are also a good way to keep cats out of the babies' crib. Personally I think a better way of keeping cats out of a crib is to not have cats. And if your kid can teach himself to unzip a crib net? Let them go; they've earned their freedom.

The Five Stages of Toddler Bedtime

Denial: Bedtime? That's ridiculous. I am not even going to entertain the notion that it would possibly be anywhere near time for bed. Obviously we just woke up like twelve hours ago. That's so funny that you would even say something so insane. I am laughing really hard right now. I'm just going to pretend you never said anything about it. Let's put this momentary ugliness behind us and continue on with our TV show.

Anger: ARE YOU HIGH, WOMAN? I am not going to bed. Not, not, not, not, not going to bed. I know you don't want to mess with me. You've seen what I can do. Look at this face. Do I look happy? This is not going to end well. I'm going to start screaming right now and I'm not going to stop until you let me stay up later!

Bargaining: Listen. I can see you're serious. How about

this: I'll watch the rest of this show and then just one more and then we have fifteen stories and a glass of water and then I will 100 percent go to bed. Cool? Wait, I can't go to bed! My stomach hurts! I'm hungry. If you give me a snack first I promise I will go!

Depression: Wow. I didn't think you would do me like this. Two measly stories? I have no words. Why did you even have me if you were just going to put me to bed with two stories? What's the point? I don't know anymore. I guess I'll just lie here and cry quietly and hope you feel guilty enough to come to your senses.

Acceptance: This. Is. Actually. Happening. No one is coming for me. Nothing else to do except drift off I suppose. Okay, fine. Sure, I will sleep well, Mom and Dad. Thanks. You sleep well too! You're going to need it. Because just for this I will see you at five a.m. Motherfuckers!

The thing to remember is that no matter what's going on with your kids and sleep, take heart. It *is* a phase. I know it may feel terrible and like it will always be this way. Believe me, I can relate to that. I can't help but worry that whatever is going on in my life is the new normal. If I have a migraine it's impossible to remember a time when I didn't feel like a machete was wedged between my ears; if I'm unemployed, I can't recall when I ever bought a new T-shirt without fear of losing my house. But trust me when I say that you will sleep again. And guess what! Someday soon (*since it supposedly all goes so fast, right?*) our babies will be teenagers—inert sixteen-year-old slugs who want to sleep until noon rather than get up and help rake the leaves or give us a ride to the drugstore to get us some more Depends. And when these rascally teens try to sleep in, we can go into their rooms at six a.m. and wake their asses up! And when they whine, "What the hell? What are you doing? Are you crazy?" we can say, "Payback's a bitch."

Kids' Bedtime Excuses

1. There's a fly in my room.

2. Well, what time are you going to bed?

3. There's no ice in my water and I clearly stated that I wanted ice water.

4. This is the wrong cup for my water.

5. I think one of my knees is bigger than the other.

6. My lips are chapped.

7. The tag in my jammies is bothering me.

8. "I'm having a bad dream." "But you haven't fallen asleep yet." "Touché."

9. I think someone stole my blankie.

10. My feet itch.

11. I'm wondering when we can go to Disneyland again.

12. My hair feels funny.

13. I'm worried that kangaroos bite.

14. Am I allergic to anything?

15. Can I have dessert again?

16. I want to sleep in your room.

17. You forgot to tuck me in.

18. My brain is telling me funny jokes and I need to share them with you.

19. My lamp is too loud.

20. My socks are too tight.

21. There's a penny in my bed.

22. I can't figure out why pudding is so delicious.

23. I forgot what comes after twenty-nine.

24. It's not dark enough outside.

25. My legs are hot.

ABC: Always Be Closing

W ay back when I was eighteen and realized that I probably would not be going off to college due to the combo platter of "2.3 GPA," "low SAT scores," and "zero extracurricular activities to put on college application," I knew that in order to succeed in life I would need a shortcut. And I found it in the exciting world of Kirby vacuum cleaner sales.

After spotting a classified ad, which promised huge commissions plus unlimited bonus opportunities, I was positive it was only a matter of time before I was hiring a Realtor to show me around some choice properties in Northern Cal (wine country) and telling my old high school nemesis (who am I kidding, nemeses) to suck it. I signed up and went to a two-day seminar on how to be become a super-successful vacuum cleaner salesperson, where I learned how to close some deals by overcoming objections, getting prospects to answer questions with a "yes" response, and maintaining a PMA—positive mental attitude. Most important was the golden rule, to remember my ABCs: always be closing.

Unfortunately, after a week in the vacuum biz, I'd exhausted all my leads and developed a decidedly NMA— negative mental attitude. I soon abandoned my sales career in favor of a much less risky venture: playing the lottery.

Little did I know, once I became a parent, I'd be thrown right back into the fire when I entered the über-competitive world of fund-raising for my kids.

Schools love to fund-raise. Even private schools that need money like Snooki needs a tan seem to have fund-raisers every twenty minutes. Who could have predicted the amount of time we parents would be required to spend harassing relatives, neighbors, and friends to buy everything from raffle tickets to World's Finest candy bars to magazine subscriptions? *Popular Mechanics*, anyone? Exactly. I've heard of friends having to go door-to-door selling wrapping paper. In May! Isn't that sort of like opening a snow-shoveling service in the summer? Or a Halloween store in July? I could go on. And on.

I get that schools need stuff. I'm not under any delusions that the teachers are skipping off to Vegas to shove dollar bills in some dude's sweaty G-strings at the Thunder from Down Under show with the money that parents brought in from selling blobs of frozen cookie dough. I know our schools need desks and chairs and pencils, but this selling shit is challenging even to a seasoned sales professional like myself.

My first year at my kid's charter school, I was super down with the cause and hit the ground running. I dutifully bought T-shirts, magnets, and mugs, and dragged my kid (and the twins, who were impossible toddlers at the time) to the Fall Festival—where I put my sales experience to use manning the bake sale table for a few hours. (I may or may not have been accused of sneaking a few Rice Krispies treats, which I hotly denied at the time, but I feel now would be an opportune time to come clean: yeah, I ate a few, okay? But the Rice Krispies treats were the kind with peanut butter! What if there were kids with allergies there that day? I took one for the team in the name of safety! You're welcome!)

As these things go, by the time the big end-of-the-year gala rolled around, I'd already shot my wad and was completely burned out, but the school's biggest and boldest fund-raiser was just kicking off: Every family was expected to sell at *least* fifty tickets to a wine raffle. Unfortunately, I had quit drinking years before, and it just seemed awkward to sell wine to my friends and family; also, it's not exactly the type of thing your child can go sell door-to-door—unless you're a fan of impromptu visits from CPS. In a fit of desperation, I briefly considered taking the tickets to an AA meeting: "Listen, congratulations on your ten years of sobriety, but we all know that most people don't stay sober forever, so on the off, off chance that you go back to drinking, why not have some delicious wines on hand instead of that Two-Buck Chuck, amirite?" In the end, I just did what most people do and bought all the tickets myself, and then prayed I didn't win so I wouldn't end up drunk in a gutter somewhere surrounded by twelve empty bottles of fine Chilean Shiraz yelling, "I did it for the children!"

I would have just given back the raffle tickets, but the problem is that after all the pep rallies and assemblies you feel bad if you don't buy the tickets, "designer jewelry," coupon books, etc. and your kid gets left out of the class Popsicle party, Jamba Juice gift card, or flashlight-that-looks-like-a-pen prize.

Again, I'm not opposed to pulling out my wallet if it's for a good cause like school. But you know who can bite me?

The effing Girl Scouts. As if we parents don't have enough product to push for our kids' education, if your kid joins Girl Scouts you're screwed. I learned the hard way that these bizzotches are all about cookie sales. My daughter's first meeting felt more like an Amway convention when a Girl Scouts "rep" came to talk to the moms about cookie sales.

"Cookie sales are the biggest moneymaker of the year," she said. "The girls can easily earn four thousand dollars!" What she didn't mention was that the troop only earns a few cents a box, while the Girl Scouts organization and the cookie manufacturer get the rest. According to the cookies' website, if your child sells cookies, she will acquire these skills: goal setting, decision making, money management, people skills, and business ethics. Yeah, well maybe the parents will, because that's who's doing the selling, and as I found out, it's a shit-ton of work, contrary to the rep's assertion that the "cookies sell themselves!" Really? Do the cookies actually drive their little minty behinds over to cookie headquarters, pick up the rest of their friends, and head on over to stores, street corners, and office buildings, where they shamelessly hawk themselves for hours on end? Do their little peanut butter fingers fill out the paperwork, persuade diabetics to buy three boxes "for the troops," and then pile themselves into a minivan and distribute themselves when the shipment comes in?

I highly doubt it.

For one thing, I've never seen a box of cookies in a little green beret. But to be fair, I bet it would look cute, especially the Savannah Smiles. The truth is, the parents do all the heavy lifting. Some parents have it easy because they can sell the cookies at work. This year one dad from my kids' troop moved 175 boxes in a week when he sold them outside of his medical marijuana dispensary. Too bad none of our girls were allowed to be selling there, because that's the kind of lesson in "business ethics" I could get behind.

Unfortunately, since I work from home, our selling went about as well as the Kirby vacuum cleaners expedition, and I now have twenty unsold boxes of Girl Scouts cookies by my front door that I was forced to buy myself. Samoas, anyone?

Hoarders

What's wrong with children? Why can't they get rid of anything ever? Why did my twins build an intricate city (replete with its own zoo) out of multiple variety packs of Play-Doh modeling compound and then leave it on our living room coffee table for three months until it was dried out and crumbling, forcing us to limit all of our socializing to other people's houses? Why does their closet contain every pair of shoes they've owned since birth? Why does our bathroom look like a youth hostel because the kids have somehow managed to acquire over seventeen toothbrushes each? Oh, you think it's just me? Uh-uh.

Go take a look around your house. It's a wreck. Seriously. There are half-built Lego structures everywhere! You can't even walk through a single room without fear of injury. "What the hell are you talking about?" you might be saying. "We *maybe* have one set of Legos! Two at the most!" Sweetie, you're in denial, which is probably for the best. It's just nature's way of protecting us from the truth, because if we were forced to constantly take in the depths of the clutter it might send us straight into a psych unit for a little court-mandated downtime.

"How dare you! You don't know me! You don't know my life!" Shhh. Shhh. Take it easy! It's okay. No one's blaming you. In fact, we're all in the same boat!

Here's the thing: It's not our fault. It's our children; they're hoarders. It's true. All of our children have the severe psychological problem of hoarding. Yet for some reason, I've yet to see even one child featured on the show *Hoarders*. And don't bother writing to the producers over at A&E about it. You will not get a response. I've tried and tried. What is the problem? I guess you have to know someone. Hollywood!

Left to their own devices, kids' rooms will overflow with useless shit. They cannot throw anything away, ever. Children don't know what trash cans are for. If they can't manage to toss out the wrapper from their Nutri-Grain bar, how can we expect them to throw away their treasured belongings? Any child whose room is organized is only that way because they have a parent with OCD, not because any child anywhere has ever felt the spirit move them to put anything back in the right place. Go into their room right now and take a quick tour. Look on their bookshelves. Do you see that yellowing booklet? That's not a children's book. That's a "Welcome to Karate" brochure that your kid saved from the one time eight years ago that you thought it would be fun to take them to a course offered through the park. Of course, the place was chaotic, and the sensei clearly had a drinking problem, so you never went back, but the pamphlet will live on the bookshelf forever. Your daughter may have been out of Girl Scouts since before you started dying your grays, but she's saved every patch and pin, her vest, and assorted swaps. Not to mention the left-over Thin Mints that didn't sell. Not that I'm complaining about that last one.

Oooh, there's a Ziploc baggie with a broken barrette, four pencils that are missing erasers, and some decomposing Easter chocolate (do not under any circumstances eat the choc—oops, too late). Next go into your kid's closet. This is helpful on two fronts: 1) you will find a lot of crap to toss that they will never in a million years miss and 2) there is the possibility that you will find some pot your child was trying to hide from you. Now you can confront your child and get them the help they need, *and* you can smoke their weed since this process is making you incredibly tense anyway!

Since we've established that a caring psychologist employed by A&E isn't going to come to your house and help you figure out what is simply clutter and what is okay to save for another few months, I am here to help. Also, you can't leave any of these decisions up to your children because they will scream bloody murder at each broken toy you try to sneak out the back door.

Goody bags are your enemy: Do not let these into your house! When your kid takes home a goody bag from a birthday party, you need to throw it out before you even get out of the car. Your kids may put up a fight, but the truth is most will have eaten the candy and lost the Super Ball under the front seat before you've even pulled into your driveway. Chances are good that they won't care about the Chinese finger cuffs or the plastic spinning top. And if the goody bag contains, God forbid, a live fish or hermit crab or some other thing that people who have super over-the-top parties and no sense sometimes send home with small children, for heaven's sake release that shit into the wild before you go inside!

Throw out all of your kids' games: Yes, you heard me. Candy Land? You don't need it. Apples to Apples? Please. Your kids got that as a gift and opened it before you could stash it away in the "regifting closet." Then they played it once, at which time over half of the cards didn't make it back in the box. You're still finding them under couch cushions and in kitchen cabinets, and every once in a while you stand up and one of them is stuck to your ass. How about Sorry!, you ask!? It can't be played anyway, since half the colors are missing one or more of their game pieces. The last time you played it you were forced to use a hemorrhoid insert as a stand-in for the yellow guy. I'm kidding, you've never actually played it! Look, if worst-case scenario your kid gets a wild hair up their ass to play Candy Land, you can go rebuy it. Candy Land will only cost you about $7.99 to replace. Think about it: isn't it worth $7.99 to not have piles of unused crap that your kids never use and won't miss?

Sell or donate books: Look, I'm pro reading. You already know this about me. But your house doesn't need to have all the books! What are you trying to

prove? We get it, your kids looove reading. But seeing as how your twins are twelve, do you really need
to hold on to the entire series of Touch and Feel
books? Be honest with yourself, is your fourteen-
year-old still reading *Pat the Bunny*? If so, put down
this book and get your child some help!

Toss out entire bins: You may have done your IKEA-
inspired best to keep some semblance of order, and I
applaud you for that. But those pathetic plastic bins
that are "organizing" your playroom? There is nothing
you need in there. Don't even bother looking through
them. What's the point? Here, I'll tell you what's in
them and save you the trouble: they're mainly full of
McDonald's Happy Meal toys. Oh, sure, you may also
find an American Girl doll cheerleader pom-pom, a
few naked old Barbies who haven't looked good since
American Idol was relevant, wheels, a sock, and your
diaphragm. Oh my God, your diaphragm! There it is!
You've been looking all over for that! Aren't you glad
you listened to me? You're welcome!

Round-file all puzzles: Puzzles are good for children's brains. No one is arguing that. And no one is
saying that kids shouldn't do puzzles, but I am saying

they shouldn't be doing them in your home. If your child's public school wants to take responsibility for a one-thousand-piece jigsaw puzzle, that's their funeral, but don't let your kids turn your house into a cardboard wasteland. Just walk around and throw every puzzle in the trash. Face it, most of them are missing pieces anyway, which will only lead to your kids' frustration.

Release stuffed animals back into the wild: And by "the wild," I mean your Dumpsters. There is no need to share your limited square footage with nine hundred stuffed animals! And sure, your kids will protest that they have a special bond with each and every one of them, including the miniature lamb that fell off the mobile that hung over their crib when they were an infant. They love that one most of all! Bullshit. Toss them out little by little until only the truly necessary ones remain. Or you can have a pretend lice scare, bag them all up, drag them into the garage, and then forget about them.

ADVANCED

Go into the garage: Why do you still have an Exer-Saucer? Your "baby" is nineteen. I'm sorry to be the one to tell you this, but you are never going to get your shit together to have that garage sale you keep talking about having. So go back in the house and call the Salvation Army to come do a pickup. Let them take everything.

Why Do They Call It Volunteering
If It's Mandatory?

I don't know if you've noticed this, but parents are expected to be a hell of a lot more involved at their kids' schools than when we were kids. When I was little, I set an alarm, got up, got dressed, ate a piece of toast, and walked myself to the bus stop while my parents were still asleep. The only time my parents made an appearance at my school was if there was a concert or play (and even that was not a sure thing). Hang on, before you reach for a tissue to dab your tears, it wasn't just me; no one's parents were hanging around. And if my mom and dad did show up for anything, it was like the best day of my life! The other kids would stare at me with sad jealous eyes like we all lived at a big old orphanage and I'd just been chosen by a forever family.

But times have changed. Nowadays, lots of parents

wake their kids up in the morning, make them some sort of nutritious breakfast, drive them to school, and then *never leave*. Not only are parents encouraged to show up for each and every play, project, party, and spelling bee, they're expected to volunteer a lot of their time. And it sucks.

The amount of meetings, field trips, library periods, school events, and in-classroom work where volunteers are needed is insane. I sort of understand it with public schools, where they're understaffed and there isn't enough money to sustain all the extras that parents demand these days, but what about private schools where people pay tuition? You'd think those people could buy themselves a break. If I were paying thirty grand a year for my kid to attend second grade I'd expect the school to buy its own art supplies. (And those art supplies? Better be worthy of Michel-fucking-angelo. Seriously, what the hell is up with schools that cost 30K? If I'm paying that much money, they should be volunteering to do shit for me, like giving me mani/pedis and raking my lawn. But I digress . . .)

A lot of schools actually require you to log a certain number of volunteer hours per kid, per school year. Which obviously begs the question: why do they call it volunteering if it's mandatory? Seriously. It's not a rhetorical question. I wish someone could explain it to me. At many schools, you have to fill out paperwork at registration that tells the administration your interests and hobbies so they can find areas for you to help in and committees for you to chair. Of course all this does for people like me is highlight how awful it would be if I had to fill out an online dating profile! I'm boring and have no hobbies! The school doesn't care though. No matter how lame your interests are, they'll find a way to put you to work: *Do you think flowers are pretty? Well maybe you'd enjoy chairing the campus beautification committee! Ever sewn a button? Great! You can be in charge of making costumes for the high school musical! Oh, you've never sewn a button? That's fine, you can co-chair.* Don't even think about mentioning your passion for organizing, because you will find yourself with a full-time unpaid position e-mailing the weekly newsletter and making copies in the school office. It's a wonder any parent can hold down outside employment or a marriage.

Basically moms are divided into two types of people: those who want to be room parents and those who would never in a million fucking years even think about it. Some of us tried being a room parent in preschool and found out the hard way what a competitive, thankless job it is. And others started out in preschool, became addicted to the power, and have been hard-core every year since. And trust me, those ladies *live for this shit*. They have never met a committee they haven't wanted to chair, a project they didn't want to "take the lead on," or an e-mail chain they didn't want to be cc'd on. And the rest of us, compared to them, are slackers.

But have you noticed that the moms who are on every committee and basically live at school often act like they *have* to do it or it just won't get done? They never fail to find a passive-aggressive way to tell you about it. "Oh, I'm fine taking all the pictures for the yearbook every year; after all, I'm at every single event anyway! It's really not a problem because my child is my full-time job!"

They say that 20 percent of the parents do 80 percent of the work. But what they never mention is that those 20 percent spend a lot of time bitching about the other 80 percent. And some of those 20 percenters can be real assholes to those of us who are just *trying to do our part to fill in the gaps on the missing 20 percent!*

Okay, fine, so maybe I'm a little defensive. I admit there was a time, before I had truly become acquainted with my limitations, when I attempted to be a full-on 20 percenter. When my first daughter started kindergarten at a charter school, I found out that parents were required to volunteer for fifty hours a year. I figured I'd hit the ground running by showing up for a preliminary meeting for parents who had expressed an interest in being on the raffle committee for the big spring fund-raiser. And not to sound cocky, but I wasn't sweating it. At all. How hard could it be to handle collecting a few raffle items? After all, I myself had volunteered to co-chair the silent auction at my kids' preschool, although I'd been forced to resign because of some ugliness regarding my not being able to figure out how group e-mails work, which resulted in the school not getting some semi-important information like the date and time of the event. But, *whatever*, that was *so* one year ago. I had Gmail now, so things were obviously going to be different.

We met at some tables in the courtyard, and I immediately sensed trouble. A couple of the moms had brought coffee and a spread of baked goods to this "meeting before the actual meeting," and they weren't even on the hospitality committee. It was ridiculous! I was already getting shown up by volunteers who weren't even actually volunteering to volunteer yet. And these bitches even had the nerve to remember napkins and coffee stirrers!

I should have realized right then and there I was in over my head, but I naively figured that once I had my marching orders, I could get things done my way, i.e., on the couch, sending out a few e-mails while watching reality television. It didn't work out that way. I was bombarded by sixty e-mails a day, subjected to conference calls to discuss whether or not I'd managed to do the things I was asked to do on earlier conference calls, and expected to generate leads for raffle items at the staggering pace of every single day. I hadn't worked this hard when I had an actual job. Which could explain my somewhat spotty work history.

Here's the thing: people expect you to stay interested in these school projects 24/7, day after day, all the way up through the actual event. Who's got that kind of attention span? Some nights, I couldn't even get through an entire episode of *Teen Mom* before I got too tired and had to go to bed. This is no way to live!

I wish I could say that I established some personal boundaries, like telling everyone on the committee, "I don't give a shit if the baskets at Michael's are only on sale until midnight, I'm not going over there at eleven thirty p.m.," or saying, "Can we *please* cap the e-mails at eighty-five per day?" No, I'm much better at avoiding confrontation and storing up resentments. So I just suffered in silence and made it through the event. But I did take away a lesson from that experience. Like, for instance, I learned that I'm not really a "team player." I'm kidding. I already knew that about myself. Here's the thing I really did learn: not every-body is good at everything.

My advice is to find a few things you're good at and just stick with that. Volunteering is like Internet dating; you have to be choosy or you'll end up wasting everyone's time. There is no need to be mixing it up at your kid's school all day long if that isn't your thing. And if it makes you feel bet-ter, most kids don't really want their parents hanging out at their school all the time anyway. Sure, your kindergart-ner might think it's cool the first time, but more than that is overkill. Do you really want to be the clingy, needy mom on the outside that you know you are on the inside? So find some other ways to help. Are you good at writing checks? Great! Most schools seem to love money! Are you awesome at grant writing but you must be at home, four wineglasses in, to really get your groove on? Excellent! No one needs to know! Can you bake like a motherfucker? Then bring your stuff to the bake sale and then back the hell away! Do you have a way to get Bill Gates to come and speak at your kid's middle school graduation ceremony? Well, what are you waiting for? Lock that shit down and then take the next four years off! You are done!

Look, we all know that giving time to our kid's school is vitally important; our schools can't run without us. But we also need to learn to not be a pussy and how to say no, or we will wind up doing everything. I've learned this the hard way, and now I'm telling you. The problem is, if you waver and show weakness, the people who do the organizing will smell your fear of confrontation and need to please from a mile away, and you *will* find yourself heading up the annual giving committee, personally snapping every yearbook photo, organizing the Jog-a-Thon, running the third-grade juice bar, designing hoodies for the track team, and bringing home the class iguana. And that will just be Monday.

So don't be embarrassed to say no to volunteering when you aren't cut out for it or if you have some other really lame reason like, oh, maybe you work eighty hours a week researching alternative cancer treatments, or you're the president. But if you are too embarrassed to just say no, here are a few surefire ways to avoid ever being asked again.

How to Avoid Being Asked to Volunteer

- Demand high fives because you finally cleared a background check.

- When discussing the next fund-raiser wonder loudly if McDonald's caters.

- Send out an e-mail about your idea to shoot a "Hot Husbands of the PTA" calendar and state your intention to hold private auditions in your home.

- Go to a committee meeting and say, "I'm sorry, but that's not how we did things when I worked at Hooters."

- Ask that people refer to you by your nickname: Lice Magnet.

- At the next committee meeting yell, "We could all learn a thing or two about teamwork from those ladies on Dance Moms!"

- Three words: multiple facial piercings.

- Get caught leaking the secret passcode to the office copier. Be unrepentant.

- Attempt to start a Peanut Allergy Deniers committee.

Don't Tell Me I'm Doubly Blessed

H ave you noticed that everywhere you look these days people are popping out twins? Having a singleton (that's what they're called in the multiples biz) went out in the nineties and now twins are *in, baby*. Oh yeah, a set of babies is the latest trend right up there with Pomeranians and the color orange. Just grab an issue of *US Weekly* and you'll see that all the cool celebrities are doing it: Julia Roberts, Angelina Jolie, Rebecca Romijn, Mariah Carey, J. Lo, Sarah Jessica Parker, Celine Dion, Nancy Grace, Denzel, Jenna Jameson, Patrick Dempsey—even Shakespeare had twins (dude has always been ahead of his time)! I could keep going but I'm a little busy because I myself have *twins*!

The occurrence of twins is up to one in thirty births

from one in fifty in 1980. That's, like, almost double! *What is up with that?* you might be thinking. Well, according to the two seconds of research I just did, the explanation for this massive twins explosion is twofold: For one, women are waiting until they're super old to start a family these days, and it seems that God has this super-hilarious joke going where as you get older, your body starts dropping eggs like it's having a going-out-of-business sale. So just when you're almost too old to have more babies, you get a two for one. *Dos por uno*, as they say in LA. This is what happened to me. Basically, my eggs were like legwarmers left over from 1983 that my body finally realized it was never going to wear, so why not push them out all at once? Which, note to God, makes no sense whatsoever because we older moms are way too exhausted to be dealing with twins! No disrespect, God, but you got this shit totally backward. Couldn't you have stuck the teen moms with the higher chance of twins and left us sleepy seniors to just the one? Come on, teens are used to staying up all night!

The other reason is that many more women are using fertility drugs and treatments to get knocked up (possibly due to having waited until they're older; it's the old, "Oops, I forgot to have a baby" phenomenon), and those drugs and treatments increase the risk of turning your womb into a human Pez dispenser.

The only problem with twins' no longer being an oddity is now that it's so common, people on the street will just walk right up and try to engage us "twins moms" in conversation about it, rather than avoiding eye contact like we have a facial rash, which I'd find far more comfortable. Maybe that's just me.

All I can say is, if you are going to approach a mom of twins, especially a new mom, let me take some time out of my busy schedule of raising too many children to give you a few conversational pointers or, more accurately, things not to say:

1. "You're doubly blessed." I know you mean well, but not every mom of twins is brimming over with joy at all the extra work involved in managing two babies at once. They might be feeling overwhelmed, and your saying how "blessed" they are will only add to the guilt they might be putting on themselves for, well, possibly feeling cursed. I'd venture a guess that 99.9 percent of the people who whip out this cliché don't actually have twins and thus have no idea what they're talking about. The other .1 percent are probably heavily medicated.

2. "They're twins? Really? They look so . . . different." Okay, this is one I get all the time because my twins are very different in height and weight so, fine, maybe I'm being oversensitive here, but how do you expect a person to respond to this? "Oh, shit. You know what? I may have walked out of the hospital with an extra baby! Not again!" If you don't want a sarcastic response, just take our word for it and don't mention it.

3. "Did you conceive them naturally?" Every mom of multiples has been forced to field this question . . . multiple times. Look, I have no problem with the question if you're actively going through fertility treatments or if you're another mother of twins, but the random looky-loo can STFU. Mainly because I didn't use fertility drugs, and so then I have to inform you that my husband and I did it, which leads into the whole "older women are more likely to have twins thing," and then we all stand around awkwardly until I have to pretend like something "urgent" has just come up on my cell phone and run for the hills. As if talking with a stranger about what goes on in my vagina wasn't already uncomfortable enough.

4. "Do twins run in your family?" Seems innocent enough, right? The problem for me is that if I say no, it invariably leads the questioner right back to question number three. And ain't nobody got time for that.

5. "I know how you feel, because my kids are only a year apart so it's exactly like twins." No, it's actually not. I'm not underestimating how difficult it would be to have a baby and then find yourself with another one a year later, but it's *your own damn fault*! You knew how brutal it was to have a newborn, yet somehow you were cocky enough to play it fast and loose with your birth control. If you're managing to have sex with a three-month-old lounging next to your bed in a Moses basket, then quite frankly you had this coming. Do they make Moses basket bunk beds, by the way? Someone should look into this. One addendum to this: if your kids are eighteen months apart and you say it's "exactly like twins," expect a dirty look because, chile, please!

6. "Were you trying to have twins?" I'm not a fertility doctor because of a little snafu with medical school (I didn't go), so I don't know *exactly* how IVF works, but I'm guessing that doctors don't just toss a few more embryos in the ol' uterus because they're *trying* to get you twins. Unless of course they're treating the Octomom. Then all bets are off.

7. "Oh God, if I had twins I would die." It's not a car accident; it's one more child. You wouldn't die; you'd adjust. You'd cry a lot for sure, and your hair would start sprouting grays like some sort of octogenarian Chia Pet, but you'd eventually get used to it the same way I had to, and the same way millions of people have to every day. Now buy me a sandwich.

8. "I always wanted to have twins!" So there you are watching a new mom struggle with her double stroller unable to get the behemoth through the front doors of Starbucks, where she will end up being forced to buy her kids cookies or listen to them scream "I want cookies" for half an hour, and you want to stop her to let her know that if you were in her position, you'd be super excited? Dude, not cool. If you want to make up for it, you know what you should do instead? Hold the fucking door open for her!

9. "I bet you never ever have sex anymore." No one's actually said this to me out loud, but I'd bet my house that you've said it in your head. And anyway, you're wrong. A few times a year is hardly *never*.

10. "How is it possible that you had twins? You look amazing!" Hold on, did I say *don't* say this? I mean, *say this*! And then repeat it a few times. And then say, "Has anyone ever told you that you look like a slightly hotter version of Angelina Jolie?" It's a terrific icebreaker. Other terrific icebreakers include: "I had to walk over and tell you that I've never seen such well-behaved kids in a restaurant!" and "Can I buy you a massage?"

Disclaimer: All of this depends on our mood. Many of us twins' parents are just grateful that someone is talking to us. Anyone. And we will gladly overlook a dumb comment if it means getting to enjoy a moment of adult conversation. But other times, not so much. Give us a break. We're overworked and undercaffeinated.

What's Mine Is Mine:
Why Sharing Sucks

Parents waste a lot of time trying to force their kids to share. At any given time at any given park you will hear a chorus of moms and dads yelling things like, "Django! Hey, buddy, can you let that other little boy use your shovel?" and "Elsa, give your friend some of your Goldfish crackers!" Despite the fact that Django may want to say, "I just got this shovel! Get your own damn shovel," and Elsa might be thinking, *I'm supposed to just let that little vagrant reach into my Goldfish crackers? Those hands look like she hasn't washed them since she was in diapers!*, we, as a society, still expect the kids to share. We figure it's the civilized thing to do, and when our kids are polite and have good manners, it reflects well on us as parents. I get it. Look, I'm all for trying to fool people into thinking I'm great at parenting, but I've decided that forcing little kids to share may be setting our sights too high.

By the time my twins were fourteen months old, they were already forging World War II–level battles over toys, attention, blankets, and food. I'm pretty sure if left to their own devices they would have fought to the death over a yogurt-covered blueberry that rolled under the kitchen counter. It's a good thing I didn't keep any weaponry lying around the house or it would've been every baby for herself.

The only family member even more put out by the twins than me was their big sister: when one of the babies grabbed for her toys, she'd scream like she was being mugged at knifepoint—"No! Stop! That's mine!" Of course, my first reaction was always to ask her to share, and when she invariably flipped out I'd do what any mom would and try to work out some sort of compromise. This usually solved the problem about 0 percent of the time. But if I'd actually stopped for ten seconds and looked at it from her point of view, I might have been more understanding. Sharing sucks. Adults don't like to do it either!

Imagine how you would feel if you bought a brand-new dress and your friend came over and said, "Oooh, I love your dress! Let me wear it!" And you said, "Sorry, I just got it! I haven't even worn it yet! The tags are still on it!" and then your mom came out and said, "Honey, don't be rude! Let your friend wear your dress! She thinks it's pretty!" and then when you started to get upset your mom came up with this genius plan: "Okay, tell you what, you wear it for five minutes and then she gets to wear it for five minutes. I'll set the timer." Yeah, you'd be sitting in a corner crying in your pantyhose, too.

The problem is we try to force our kids to share when it doesn't come naturally to them. Babies are not able to share at all, so if you're trying to get your one-year-old to give something up that they like to another child, you may as well beat your head against a brick wall for ten minutes. Either way, the results will be the same. The baby won't share and you'll end up needing something prescription strength for your headache.

Around the age of two or three, toddlers start to get the concept, but that doesn't mean they want to do it. These kids practice something called "proto-sharing," which is where they will show an object to another child and let the other child fondle it, but they won't actually let it go. This may look selfish when your kid does it, but if you think about it, grown-ups do that same shit all the time. Ever see a guy get a new car and drive it over to his buddy's house to show it off? "Dude, I got a Tesla. This thing can drive from Los Angeles to China on a single charge! Hop in, I'll take you for a spin!" The other guy will undoubtedly ask, "Can I drive it?" and he'll say, "By yourself? Are you high?" See what I mean?

Granted, there are times when all kids need to share— like when they have a friend over to play and the other kid's parents don't think to bring the kid's entire collection of toys with them so their kid has something to do. At those times, we as parents have to make sure our kid does the right thing, because otherwise we will never get to sit on the couch with *our* friends to discuss *Game of Thrones*.

I'm not saying that sharing isn't important; it is part of having friends and getting along with others. I'm just saying that maybe we don't need to force our kids to do it *all the time*. In fact, the next time I'm at the park and another kid hops on my kid's bicycle, I may not be so quick to insist that she "be nice and take turns." I may just tell her that it's okay to say, "Sorry, but that's mine." I mean, if I don't know you and you decide to take my Prius for a spin around the neighborhood, we don't call that sharing, we call it grand theft auto. Why should it be different for our kids?

If I am trying to raise self-assured, confident daughters, how is teaching them to be total pushovers by letting anyone walk up and grab their stuff going to further my cause? I read once that kids who take a stand about not sharing are actually showing signs of a healthy self-esteem. So rather than freak out when my kids don't want to share, I'm going to tell myself that I'm doing my part to raise future leaders! And then keep my head down and try not to make eye contact with the other moms at the park.

Read 'Em and Weep

I'm going to let you in on a little secret that you will not read in other, less ballsy parenting books: getting your kids to love reading can save you a buttload of money on college. Yeah, I said that. I'm crazy controversial! I'm in your face! But I'm telling you the truth. Kids who love to read will sail through grade school, middle school, and high school and can probably skip college altogether—or maybe that's just me.

My husband would be extremely irritated if he thought I was advocating skipping college, so let me clarify: I'm not saying you should skip college (even though you would avoid hefty student loans and a probable Adderall addiction), I'm just saying that if for some reason you didn't go to college you might find that you can still eke out a decent living based solely on having read a ton of books. And having rich parents.

Hey, I don't have to tell you that reading is great; look at you, you're reading right now! Unless of course I recorded an audio version of the book and you're listening to me read it to you. But let's not split hairs here. I think you get what I'm talking about.

Unfortunately this is yet another area of parenting where we have to actually do something. Developing a love of reading starts with us sitting down every night and reading to our kids; obviously they don't just pop out of the womb knowing how to read (except for certain prodigy babies; see "They Can't All Be Gifted," page 43) but I believe it's totally worth it. A whole lot of studies have shown that kids who are read to consistently have better attention spans, bigger vocabularies, and are more likely to do well in all aspects of education. It's really one of the best things you can do for your kid! *Yeah! I said it's one of the best things you can do for your kid! So suck it, breast-feeding!*

And the benefits of reading go beyond young kids. Older kids who love reading will be armed with a built-in escape from the hardships in their lives—you know, like when you refuse to let them get their ears pierced or when they accidentally wipe out the roller coaster they just built on SimCity. And hey, with the ability that books have to soothe, maybe kids will be less likely to turn to drugs. Ha ha ha ha!

If you are dedicated to reading to your children, then you know that it's more challenging than when we were kids. We were easier to please because we didn't have as many choices for entertainment as we have these days. Who wants to sit still for a book when there is a dizzying array of iPad apps, DVDs, and twelve episodes of *Jake and the Never Land Pirates* queued up on the DVR? Think about it: as a kid, doesn't it seem easier to just have SpongeBob scream a story at you from the TV for ten minutes than to have to sit still for a book that doesn't even have the decency to have moving pages?

Sure it's easier for the kids to do something more passive, and if we're honest, it's easier for us. Not only do we have to fight against all our children's distractions, but we have to rally against our own inherent laziness. I know that there have been countless times when I've said, "Story time," and my kids said, "Can we just watch a show tonight instead of stories?" and I've . . . well . . . caved. It takes a certain amount of inspiration to keep your book-reading enthusiasm up every single night, no matter how much you know it's important to your child's future. Sometimes you just don't feel like doing it. Hey, I know that going to the gym is important to the future of my thighs, yet it doesn't stop me from blowing it off to eat a plate of nachos and rewatch *Magic Mike*. I'm human, after all.

If you're like me, one thing that might help keep you in the mood is to step up your book collection to make sure that you have fun, interesting reads for your kids that *you* can tolerate. Especially taking into consideration that most kids, once they hear a story that catches their interest, would like to hear it fifty times in a row while you would like to check Facebook.

Remember, just because a book is a classic, it doesn't mean it won't make you want to suffocate yourself with a crib bumper! I'm sure *Goodnight Moon* seemed like a great book when I was hearing it as a toddler, but that's because there were only three channels available on TV. The book had no competition. When I went to read it to *my* kids, I realized that it's sort of snoozy and doesn't make a lot of sense: There's a bowl of mush and a comb and an old lady whispering hush. And why is she whispering hush? She's all alone! Is she an off-duty librarian? Are the socks and mittens trying to study? No? Then why do we have to hush? Listen, Grandma, go brush your damn hair and go to bed and let us do the same! Sorry, I lost it for a minute there.

I'll tell you the one that blindsided me the most: *The Story of Babar*. *Babar* is one of those books that I remembered fondly from being a kid and I was downright psyched to share with my daughter. And then I read it for the first time in thirty years and was kind of shocked and disturbed on many levels. It opens innocently enough: "In the great forest a little elephant is born. His name is Babar. His mother loves him very much. She rocks him to sleep with her trunk singing softly to him." Okay, great. But a mere two pages later, Mommy is gunned down by hunters while Babar rides on her back. Kind of more suited for a Quentin Tarantino movie, if you ask me.

Unfortunately, more unsavory lessons lie ahead. Babar scampers off to the big city, where he sees lots of new things: automobiles, streets, and—most impressively to him—finely dressed gentlemen. Out of nowhere, an old lady "who's always been fond of little elephants" hands over her purse so that Babar can go buy some new threads. Um, Babar's a gigolo! I didn't catch that plot development thirty years ago!

Need more proof? Babar moves in with her. They've known each other for like a minute and he moves in! I'm sorry, but these days we call that a cougar. She cooks him dinner every night while Babar spends his days taking baths, working out, and driving her car around the countryside. I quote: "He goes out for an automobile ride every day. The old lady has given him the car. She gives him whatever he wants." Seriously? Old lady—news flash—you are getting played! Tell Babar to get a j-o-b! This chick must have a thing for big trunks . . .

At night, Babar hangs around with the old lady's friends in his nice new clothes and regales them with stories about life in the great forest. Wouldn't that get a little grating after maybe the first night? And what kind of stories would they be? He wasn't traveling with the Ringling Bros. Circus. He was running around with no clothes, pooping everywhere, hanging with monkeys, and munching leaves for breakfast. That doesn't seem entirely scintillating to me. But apparently the old lady and her friends find it hilarious!

Then—plot twist—Babar's cousins show up. And of course, the very first thing Babar notices, since apparently he spends all his time bathing and reading *GQ*, is that they aren't wearing any clothes! I quote: "Babar kisses them affectionately and hurries off with them to buy them some fine clothes"—on sugar mama's plastic, obvi.

No sooner are the cousins decked out in new duds than their moms come looking for them, and Babar decides to bail and head back to the great forest. So Babar "the User" drives off in the old lady's car and never looks back. Oh, and since there's not enough room (why the old lady drives the equivalent of a Mazda Miata is never explained), the moms have to run behind. Nice.

Meanwhile, back in the forest, the king of all the elephants eats a bad mushroom and dies a painful death. The picture of his corpse is more gruesome than anything you'd see on *Forensic Files*. Good night, kids!

Luckily Babar returns just in time to be named the new king. But hang on, kids, there's a third-act complication: apparently, on the ride back, Babar was doing more than just watching the scenery; he was busy doing his cousin Celeste, and they've gotten engaged. I know the French think we Americans are totally bourgeois when it comes to sex with relatives, but come on.

The rest of the book is all about Babar's wedding. I find hearing about other people's weddings about as interesting as hearing about other people's bunions, so I try to skip it, but suffice it to say it ends with Babar and his cousin flying off in a hot air balloon for their honeymoon—undoubtedly bankrolled by the old lady.

Thanks, Jean de Brunhoff, but I think I'm sticking with Mo Willems for the next few years. I'll take a pigeon with an unnatural interest in driving buses over an incestuous, prostituting pachyderm any day.

Other Books We May Need to Rethink

Love You Forever: Basically an extremely codependent mom sneaks into her son's room after he's asleep and rocks him whether he likes it or not by singing him a song about how she will always love him and he'll always be her baby. The boy suffers from her invasions of privacy from babyhood until he finally leaves home and moves across town. But his intrepid mom doesn't let a pesky thing like separate residences and restraining orders stop her from singing her creepy song. She drives across town late at night, throws a ladder against the house, and climbs in his window to get her rocking on. It's supposedly a tale of motherly love. I'd say it's a tale of attachment parenting gone very very wrong.

The Giving Tree: This book is truly polarizing, and I'd fall into the camp of those who don't appreciate it. Basically a tree and a boy have a lifelong relationship in which the tree gives and the boy takes. Yes, the boy takes and takes and takes and endlessly exploits the tree, who is way too nice and needs an Al-Anon meeting.

The original Curious George: George has lots of adventures in the newer books: he goes camping, he has a birthday party, he meets firemen, he enjoys a baseball game. But the original book is a little less cheery; George is abducted from his home in Africa by the Man with the

Yellow Hat. He's tied up with ropes, put on a boat, and shipped to the big city, where he ends up in jail and then confined to a zoo. Isn't this basically the plot of *Roots*? I mean, what else is out there? The kiddie version of *Schindler's List*?

Madeline: The main plot of this story seems to be that Madeline, who lives in a group home run by nuns, gets appendicitis and has to have major surgery. She spends ten days alone in the hospital with only one visit from the other children. But apparently being alone in a hospital is better than being at the group home, because all the other kids are jealous and want to have surgery too! This thing is more depressing than a Sally Struthers infomercial.

Good Night Gorilla: I may be the only person on the planet who doesn't love this book and that's okay; I'm secure with my opinions. Here's the deal: A gorilla, who lives at the zoo, gets ahold of the zookeeper's keys and lets himself out of his cage. He then follows the zookeeper around the zoo, letting all the other animals out of their cages until they sneak into bed with the zookeeper and his wife. The problem is that the book is too complicated for the two-year-old board book market demo yet too young for kids who would get it. Plus, there's a not-so-subtle bestiality theme.

There's a Nightmare in My Closet: Yet another one I remembered fondly from my childhood, only to crack it open as an adult and be completely horrified. Hey, kids, there's a big scary monster in your closet! You're going to need to kill it with a gun! Do you have a gun? No? Oh shit! Well how the heck are you going to protect yourself against people who want to take away your freedoms, let alone rid your room of monsters? Oh well, good night. Enjoy PTSD.

Grouchy Ladybug: The poor man's *Very Hungry Cater-pillar*. In this story, the ladybug goes around acting like Charles Bukowski on a bender, yelling, "Wanna fight?" to animals a thousand times his size; (spoiler alert) eventually he ends up realizing that he cannot win and grudgingly accepts that he has to share. Nice anger management propaganda.

Every book that followed If You Give a Mouse a Cookie: If you've read one of these books, you've read them all. If you give a blank a blank, he's going to want a blank, and so on and so on until we're back to square one. It's a cute concept, but after the first one we get it. I think we're seriously at the point of diminishing returns. What's left? *If You Give an Aardvark a Valium? If You Give a Snake a Protein Shake? If You Give a Meth Head a Sudafed*?

How to Tell You're Done Having Kids

I don't know about you, but I am so done kicking out shorties. The tubes are tied, the factory is shut down, the uterus is settling in for a long winter's nap. And I couldn't be happier about it. Then again, I have three kids, which is a lot for LA; it's like having five in Idaho. Or twenty if you're on a compound in Idaho.

Now, some women know they are done having kids after the first one, while others have a second but can't figure out whether or not they want a third. And then there are the ones, like Michelle Duggar, who just don't know when to call it quits. It's like she's collecting mucus plugs for *Guinness World Records* or something. Slow your roll, Duggar.

For a long time after I had my first baby, I couldn't

decide if I wanted to have more. This isn't surprising; I've always been paralyzed by having to make big life decisions. It took me a month just to decide what color to paint my dining room. I stared at color swatches and cried, obsessed that I'd pick the wrong shade of green and live to regret my choice. Of course, I realize that having a baby is way more serious than painting a room. If you mess up your walls, you can always paint over them. Has *House Hunters* taught us nothing? Alas, you can't just paint over a baby. Well, maybe you can legally, but the baby tends to get pissy.

Usually, when I have to make big decisions, I prefer to focus-group them for a couple of years to see what everyone else is doing and, more importantly, what everyone else thinks *I* should be doing before I make a move. But you know, I didn't even give birth to kid number one until I was thirty-eight, so with this particular decision, I was under some serious time constraints. Tick tick tick!

In retrospect this was laughable and cocky considering my "advanced maternal age." My remaining eggs were so old they were hanging around at Applebee's and listening to Lawrence Welk while my uterus smoked Camels and got into the movies on a senior discount. Yet, somehow I thought I was in the driver's seat.

One of my husband's reasons for wanting to try for another was that he liked the idea of our daughter having a sibling. He thought it was important that she be part of a team, especially since we were going to be oldster parents—which I didn't appreciate being reminded about all the time. So I spent time Googling "only children" to find out whether or not having only one child would sentence her to being lonely or, worse, narcissistic and annoying. But naturally no one on any of those sanctimonious message boards ever admits to having children who are anything less than perfection, so it wasn't that helpful. I also had to consider the fact that just because you have more than one kid doesn't guarantee that they will even like each other. I myself have two siblings and only one of them is speaking to me. Just saying. It's not like the Kardashians would hang out if E! wasn't there with a camera; don't kid yourself.

I also couldn't relate to friends who knew exactly what their family plan was either. You know, the ones who are either pregnant a millisecond after they have their first kid *or* who gave birth to one; got a taste of how physically, emotionally, and financially taxing it is; and knew for sure they would be totally happy and fulfilled without more? I find that sort of lack of neurosis off-putting. What's wrong with them? Why are they so relaxed? Do they do yoga? Or worse, meditate? Freaks.

If you're currently struggling to decide whether you want more than one kid, then you know what I mean. You get it. It's a big decision, right? First off, the cons: Are you ready for another round of sleep deprivation? For some of us, the first round was life altering, and not in a positive way: I have a friend whose husband got pneumonia due to a baby who was a particularly bad sleeper and he refused to even *consider* having another baby. (Although his wife lost more sleep than he did, especially once he got pneumonia, and yet she still wanted to try for another one. What I'm saying is, he's a pussy.) Or maybe you only recently got on the right cocktail of antidepressants to deal with your extended bout of PPD. There's also the financial hardship. It's tough enough to send one kid to college; if you have a second or a third you can only pray they are serious underachievers or somehow hook up with a nice sugar daddy after they get accepted to the Ivy League. And by the way, you have to have sex to make another baby. With another person. Do you see what I'm saying? There are variables to consider.

Then again, there are plenty of reasons to go for another. I mean there is the . . . or all of the . . . I can't think of any right now, but I'm sure you can come up with a few.

In the end, we just decided, "Screw it," and, well, screwed. Sans birth control. I figured it probably wouldn't happen anyway since during all this deliberating I'd turned forty. Which is exactly how I ended up pregnant with twins. (This was fully explained in a previous chapter. See "Don't Tell Me I'm Doubly Blessed," page 177.)

When I found out I was having two more children, I practically had a stroke and then I went into a long period of denial, which was probably my body's way of protecting me from news I was too fragile to handle. I'm thinking I'll come out of it soon. Maybe when my girls turn eight.

I realize there are people who try to have three kids on purpose and I don't get those people at all. I mean, why would anyone want to have more than two kids *on purpose*? Do they just hate money and downtime? I'm not kidding. I'm not saying that China is right with trying to limit families to one kid, but I'm not saying they're wrong either.

The good news about finding out I was going from one kid to three is that there was never any question I'd need to even think about having more kids after that. And since I was having a C-sec anyway, I was able to get those loose ends tied up (so to speak) before I even left the hospital. While I was on the table, just after my little ladies had been pulled out of my ancient uterus, my doctor asked if I was sure I still wanted the tubal ligation. I guess she wondered if after having premature twins and taking them home to a chaotic house to join a toddler, I might want to reproduce again with my one remaining egg. I wondered if she was high on crack. I told her I've never been more sure of anything in my entire life, so get back in there and lock that shit down stat.

No matter how many kids you have, at some point you're going to need to call it a wrap so you can eventually get them all out of the house and move on to other hobbies. So how do you know if you're done? Here are a few signs.

You Bought New Furniture

Only people who are done having babies or are incredibly rich have the gall to buy new furniture. If you're asking why, chances are you've never met a baby. On the other hand, if you haven't bought new furniture in many years you might still be done having babies, it's just that the ones you have sucked your bank account dry.

You Got Rid of All Your Old Baby Gear

Chances are if you tossed out, sold, or gave away all your baby clothes, high chairs, blankets, and strollers, you don't want more babies. Of course, it also makes you more likely to get accidentally pregnant. #JustSaying #UseProtection #ThanksObama

You Smell Your Best Friend's New Baby and . . . Nothing

If you don't start practically lactating when you sniff the head of a newborn, this is a telltale sign that you are over the baby-making period of life. Or you're a psychopath— either way, you shouldn't have another baby. What's wrong with your soul?

You Regularly Get to Sleep Until Eight a.m. on Weekends

If you've gotten to the point where you can sleep in on weekends, life is sweet. Your kids are probably at an age where even if they wake up at seven, they can grab a bowl of cereal and work the remote. I bet you've been known to do things you haven't done since you were single and child-free, like lie on the couch for two hours eating leftover chicken dumplings and watching a Lifetime movie starring Tori Spelling. You are golden. Life is a cabaret. Don't fuck it up.

You Celebrated When Your
Youngest Was Potty Trained

If you're *that* excited by a poop in the potty, it could be because you are over potty training. And if you threw a Poopy in the Potty Party to celebrate (which, let's be honest, is an issue in and of itself), you're definitely done having babies! Entertaining is a sure sign that either you're finally done having young kids or you're parenting in the seventies and don't even know where your kids are right now.

The Idea of Baby-Proofing Is Absurd

If the only baby-proofing you plan to do is making your home inhospitable to strange babies, you don't want more kids. Be honest with yourself! I agree with you! Baby gates are an eyesore! Locks for toilets are a younger mom's game! Those rubber things that go around the sharp edges of your coffee table need to be outlawed! Do you feel strongly that the only reason to still have a gate around your pool is to keep drunk partygoers from suing? Yeah, you're not having any more kids, Chacha.

The Best Part of Holding Someone Else's
Baby Is That You Get to Give Them Back

That's a good sign you're done having kids but . . . you may be ready to be a grandparent! Geez, if I'd started having kids when my mom started having kids, I'd have a twenty-four-year-old by now. Instead, I'm just the only mom with a kindergartner and arthritis at the same time. Well, me and Halle Berry. Same thing.

Let's Not Talk About Sex

- - -- - -- - -- -- - -

You may refuse to think about it for as long as you can, but the day is going to come when you need to tell your children where babies come from. You will need to explain to them the intricate waltz of reproduction, the wonder of conception, life's greatest miracle. In other words, you're going to need to tell your kids what happens when Daddy takes the old wienermobile out for a spin. That's right, I'm talking about *sex*, baby.

I know it's awkward, and I know you don't want to even think about it, but it's something you have to do as a parent. Otherwise, how are your kids going to learn about sex? From their dumb friends? Or worse, the way they learn about everything else, by watching how-to videos on YouTube? *Wait a minute! That's not a Rainbow Loom!*

I did an unofficial polling of my friends, and it seems like most of them put this off for as long as possible. Also, people's attitudes about sex really seem to run the gamut. On one side of the spectrum, there's the uptight WASPs who make it their mission in life to avoid discussion about anything more personal than the right way to grill a steak. On the opposite side, we have the granola hippies who grew up on a commune and believe that learning to own your orgasms should start in preschool. You probably fall somewhere in the middle. Actually, let's hope you lean more toward WASP. Way more. Like tipping over more.

However, if your name is something like Honesty or Plumeria and you're the more relaxed type, just be careful. My parents taught me the facts of life early enough that I don't remember the first time I got a mental picture of the mechanics of sex. Thank God for that. On the other hand, I do remember that one night they hosted a big dinner party and in the middle of a quiet moment I asked the group, "What's a vulva?" It kind of brought the party to a screeching halt. I guess not everyone's as super relaxed as my parents were, but hey, that's the risk you run. By the way, I'm still not really clear on the definition of that word. Seriously, if you know, e-mail me.

Then there's my friend Wendi, whose WASP parents didn't tell her much at all, so when she was reading Judy Blume's *Forever* . . . and asked what a diaphragm was, they told her, "It's your rib cage," and then she tried to figure out for the next forty years how you could insert your rib cage into your vagina for birth control. Poor Wendi.

But besides the obvious awkwardness of discussing sex with kids, one of the reasons that some of us avoid telling them what's up is that we worry they won't be mature enough to handle it themselves. But according to a bunch of articles I skimmed, kids are starting to learn about this stuff earlier and earlier, and may know more than we think they know. This makes it even more important that they hear the deal straight from us.

Way before you sit down to have the actual birds-and-bees powwow, you should start by making sure your kids are using the correct terminology for their private parts. A lot of people try to use cute nicknames like "hoo hoo" or "woo woo" or "kitty kat." This is ridiculous. You want your children to know that the human body is nothing to be ashamed of, right? That's why in our house, we all refer to our girl parts with their proper name: "vajayjay"—plain and simple. And we refer to boy parts by their proper name, too: "Don't touch that until you're twenty."

So exactly what is the right age to start?

I'd say seven is perfect. The goal is to give your kids the proper information before they are fluent readers and could possibly stumble upon it themselves. Once your kid can read, you don't want to live in fear that they'll find "your friend's" copy of *Fifty Shades of Grey* that she accidentally left in the drawer in your bedside table. You would have way too much explaining to do! Like for one, why your friend is keeping her books in your bedside table!

When my daughter hit her seventh birthday, I figured this might be my last chance to make sure that she hears it from a trusted source, so we sat down and read a book called *It's Not the Stork!* When I got to the part where the man's penis has to go into the woman's vagina her response was "Ewwwww," which was exactly the response I was hoping for!

You may also want to let your child be your guide and wait until they've started asking questions. If your kid's questions are things like, "Mommy, how did the baby get in your tummy?" you don't need to get into too many details. You can keep it fairly vague: "Mommy has a seed in her body that gets fertilized by the daddy and that's how a baby starts to grow." If your child's questions are more in the vein of "What position is reverse cowgirl?" you've waited too long.

What should you say?

For the earlier conversations, start with the fundamentals, keep it simple, and get to the point in a reasonable amount of time. If you're reading a book and there are three chapters devoted primarily to getting underarm hair, you may have completely lost your kid's attention before you ever get to the money shot (sorry). That would be a big waste of time. At the same time, remember to be age appropriate. There's no need to rush right out of the gate into STDs; maybe wait a few years on the chlamydia chat so you have something to look forward to. Save that talk for something special, like prom night.

The easiest way to do this whole thing is to read from an age-appropriate book that gives you the basics but leaves room for your own personal spin on things. If you're really talented, read the book aloud to your children in a Dr. Ruth Westheimer voice.

There's also a website where you can sign up and for forty-five dollars they'll help you develop your own script and you can have practice conversations. But this seems way too over-the-top. I mean, it's not *that* hard. You shouldn't need online support; you're not going from PC to Mac or learning to do your own small-business accounting. You are simply sitting down with your kids to have an open and honest discussion about erections, wet dreams, and masturbation. On second thought, forty-five bucks seems like a sweet deal.

Hey, sorry about that, I didn't mean to scare you. It's truly not that bad. Just start young and convey the basics in a nice, neutral tone, and leave the door open for more discussions down the line. Also, it should be noted that if you have sons, you're off scot-free. Most of my friends with boys leave all penis-related issues to the dads. It's the least they can do, considering moms have to deal with all of the sticky sheets . . .

But when your kids come to you for more info, just listen and then answer their questions as simply as you can. Having given the sex talk now a few different times, I assure you that it's uncomfortable at first, but the more you do it, the easier it will be. Pretty soon you'll just be able to walk up to random kids at a frozen yogurt shop and tell them exactly how babies are made. But don't. There are laws against that. At least on the West Coast.

How to deal with sticky situations

You walk in the room and realize your six-year-old has accidentally stumbled upon something X-rated online.

What should you do? Okay, first of all, don't beat yourself up. This has probably happened to most of us at some point! It happens to my husband all the time! You wouldn't believe how many times he's tried to type in WhiteHouse.gov and accidentally typed in HornyHousewives.com! But although we all feel like we're aware enough of what our kids are doing online, the problem is the Internet is tricky. Especially YouTube! One minute your kid is happily watching a Dora and Boots video but with one click to "related content" suddenly they're seeing a Spanish woman named Dora giving oral pleasure to a dude wearing motorcycle boots. Come to think of it, I'm really not sure how exactly that is related, except for the part when a tranny named Swiper stole her tube of lube.

Anyway, if that happens, don't panic and slam the computer shut. And don't start thinking, *Jesus! I should have known this was going to happen! Why didn't I get parental controls sooner? My kid is going to be scarred for life! He'll never be able to have a normal sex life and he'll probably now have some sort of boots fetish.*

Most people don't purchase parental controls for their computer until something happens that makes them realize they need parental controls, so, hey, now you know! Chances are a random out-of-context porn sighting won't have any lasting effect on your child's psyche. But it does open the door to having a calm conversation about what activities are strictly for grown-ups and how those are not appropriate things for him to look at until he's much, much, much older. And then, coolly walk into your own bedroom and *privately* freak the fuck out.

You accidentally walk in on your child masturbating.

What should you do? For one, this most likely won't happen until they're twelve or older. Of course, there are exceptions. Everyone knows someone who has a daughter who likes to rub against things in public. But if/when you do see your child doing this, apologize and get the hell out of there. It's more embarrassing for them than for you, so there's no need to have a big discussion about it. Try buying them a Do Not Disturb sign to put on their door and leave it at that. Think of it this way: that's the safest sex they're ever going to have!

Every Teacher's Nightmare, or
How Not to Be "That" Parent

T eachers. We love them. We respect them. We know they have a hard job. After all, they are in charge of shaping our children's minds and guiding them into adulthood for eight hours a day! Hell, after just the drive to school in the car, I'm pretty much ready to clock out. So I totally get it.

Most teachers are dedicated, tireless advocates for our kids who are trying to do their best, and they deserve our appreciation. And we do appreciate the hell out of them . . . at least once a year on Teacher Appreciation Day. Although in the case of my kids' school, that shit goes on for a week, which we kind of need to talk about because Mother's Day is only one day a year—how did teachers manage to swing five? Our teachers get spa treatments, cards, coffee, flowers, scented candles, and lunches. Don't get me wrong, I love the handprints and the picture frame made out of Popsicle sticks and waffles and coffee in bed I get on my special day, but one of those thirty-five-dollar Relaxing Rituals Yankee Candles and a few hours at the Magic Hands Spa also wouldn't suck. But I digress. Teachers *rule*!

Are there any bad teachers? Of course! They can't all be Mr. Holland's Opus. Sometimes you're going to get stuck with a Mary Kay Letourneau. And even short of a *20/20* two-hour special–level bad teacher, you'll also run into the occasional burned-out PTSD case just trying to keep it together for a couple more years until retirement or a lottery scratcher pays off to deliver them from the daily torture of trying to control and educate twenty-five miniature bundles of ADD. But we have to sort of hope that most are there for the right reason, right? I mean, primary and secondary education isn't a field that typically draws people in for the fast cash, dizzying rush of power, or access to supermodels.

But if crap teachers are seemingly rare, nature seems to have provided an inexhaustible supply of insufferable, pushy, and outright nutter parents dedicated to making these educators' lives as difficult as humanly possible. Think about the odds: through elementary school at least, each year we get a single teacher to deal with for our child. They, on the other hand, are dealt dozens of us parents . . . each entrusting them with the most unique and special snowflake ever, and the colossal expectations that come with that.

You just know the teachers all hang out in the teachers' lounge, swilling vodka and orange juice out of travel mugs, trading war stories about the insane mom who got taken out of their classroom in handcuffs after she attacked a teacher with a pair of blunt-tip scissors because the teacher refused to change her son's D to a C. By the way, I'm not sure that's 100 percent accurate since the only image I have of what goes on inside a teacher's lounge is from watching *Boston Public* in early 2000, so unless that show was a documentary it's possible I may be slightly off base.

What I do know for sure is that no one wants to be "that mom." You've seen her. She's the one blocking the door to your kid's classroom every day, holding your kid's teacher hostage while she discusses all the ways the teacher can better accommodate her exceptional child. You see, her daughter, Violet, is an actress who was *just in a music video*! So she can't *possibly* do the twenty minutes a day of reading that's expected of the rest of the class. Oh, also, the book that's being read aloud by the TA before recess? Well, Violet's already heard that book and she's *bored*. Couldn't the teacher see her way clear to beef up the curriculum? *For Violet?* This kind of behavior is not going to get you on your child's teacher's good side. In fact, that teacher will at best start seeming incredibly busy whenever she sees you coming, and at worst will avoid you like you're carrying Ebola.

This can all be prevented though. First, identify the underlying cause. Many parents with enough time to lobby a teacher for thirty minutes before class, followed by twenty more of peeping through the classroom blinds, may actually be in desperate need of a hobby, or better yet, a job. Parents who work full-time are far less likely to have the hours of free time required to micromanage their kids' teachers. Although I'm sure the more extreme will make the time no matter what outside forces try to impede them.

However, a certain proportion of parents will remain unencumbered by nine-to-five employment, perpetually available to spend vast sums of time at their child's school, in close proximity to teachers. Don't get me wrong, this group also provides a great deal of good through organization and volunteer work for the school community— but let's not kid ourselves, this is also the prime breeding ground for "that parent."

In the spirit of trying to encourage some self-identification and perhaps behavior modification, here are some ways to avoid becoming a problem for your kid's teachers:

Don't do your kid's homework. At all. You can help—but helping doesn't mean doing it. Trust me, it's a lose-lose. Just see what happens when you write their essay on whether the voting age should be lowered to thirteen for them and it gets a C minus. That moment after you furiously blurt out, "But I spent hours on it!" at your parent-teacher conference will be more than a little awkward, as will be the fake phone call from the secretary of defense that you pretend to take, to cover your sudden rush from the room.

Don't be a backseat teacher. There's nothing more irritating to a teacher than when you try to suggest a better way to do their job. Got an upcoming class project on American Indians? I don't care if your family is one-quarter Apache and you once sampled elk at a friend's wedding when you were drunk; you don't know more about it than the teacher. Would you want your kid's teacher waltzing into your office at Citibank, leaning over your desk, and suggesting a better cost/benefit analysis for your client's exposure to risky investments in emerging markets? We need to trust that our teachers know what they're doing. It's their job. We've got to assume they didn't just walk off the main stage at Bob's Boobie Bungalow and say, "I'm tired of stripping, I think I'll teach third grade. I've never done it before but I have a few ideas so I'm just gonna wing it. YOLO."

Try to be on time. I mean, look, do your best, but none of us are miracle workers. When my twins first started kindergarten, one of them got marked tardy a few times because I was still trying to figure out how to get three kids to the same place at the same time every morning. When I talked to the teacher about it she said she *completely understood* how tough it must be because she herself has three dogs. I wanted to say, "Have you been sniffing the rubber cement? Because that is seriously ridiculous." But what I said was, "Oh, no way, three dogs is much harder!" On the other hand, I've seen parents drop their kids off late every. Single. Day. Like they're on Hawaiian time. Sorry, but just like a luau-print shirt, that shit is not going to fly on the mainland.

Don't be a suck-up. Obviously if you buy your kid's teacher a Starbucks coffee every morning, they will probably be happy. But don't expect special treatment. If your kid gets a bad grade you can't be like, "Bitch, I brought your ass a caramel macchiato every day, and this is the thanks I get?" Do it because you want to, not because you expect favors in return.

By the way, you aren't going to win points with the other parents. We're going to think you're up to something. We're going to go have coffee ourselves after drop-off and we're going to talk about you. I don't think either of us wants that.

If teachers need your help, they will ask for it. Volunteering to "teach" something to the class, according to quite a few teachers I've talked to, is apparently not really all that helpful. You'll come rolling in with your suggested "project" and your kid's teacher will be forced to smile and nod and say, "Oh, Civil War hand puppets? That would be . . . amazing!" All the while thinking, *Get out. Get out. Now.*

Don't try to have a serious conversation with the teacher while they're trying to teach. This one is going to really confuse a few people, but you know when you walk into your child's classroom and you see their teacher standing in front of all of those kids talking sort of animatedly, and maybe gesticulating with their hands a bit? Do you know what they're doing? Another self-check: are they using their "teacher voice" or maybe pointing at a blackboard? Are you starting to get the picture? Right! They're . . . *teaching*. So now is not a good time to chat. Most teachers prefer you to make an appointment to talk to them either before or after class. Of course if it's an emergency, then obviously you won't be able to make an appointment. And, no, the fact that your son Dodge forgot his ChapStick does not constitute an emergency. Although the fact that your son is named after a car certainly does qualify as one.

If you have a problem with the teacher, don't go over their head to the principal or administration before trying to talk to them first. Sometimes we are going to get upset at a teacher. And sometimes it will even be their fault. And we may want to go all mama bear on the situation and storm into the principal's office demanding justice. But let's be fair and try speaking to the teacher first. We may be surprised to find out that there was a misunderstanding or that the teacher was having an off day. Or we may not get anywhere and then by all means, elevate that shit. But be warned, you probably won't get far. Because thanks in part to the residual impact of generations of crazy parents, a coplike unified front between teachers and administrators has existed for decades. And now all you've done is pissed them off. Hope your kid likes getting F's. Which leads me to a related tip, which is as much for you as it is for the teachers.

Pick your battles. Not every situation is worth getting labeled "that parent" for. When one of my kids was in her first few weeks of kindergarten, her teacher got annoyed that she kept twirling in her favorite dress. The teacher apparently asked her to stop but she found it impossible to resist the pull of the twirl (apparently it's a gateway to pirouetting), and eventually her dress got expelled from the classroom permanently—which I found a bit harsh. Obviously, I considered hiring a lawyer and taking this clear violation of my daughter's civil liberties all the way to the Supreme Court if I had to. But then I realized I had to throw in a load of towels, so I decided to be the bigger person and let it slide. It ended up being a one-time thing: the teacher turned out to be awesome, and my staying calm turned out to be the best course of action all around. Also, we all had clean towels that week.

If your classroom has a policy on food such as "no cupcakes for birthdays" or "no candy with lunch," then it goes for your kid too. Regardless of your teacher's personal stance on sweets, if he has to send you back home after you try to show up with a box of baked goods for your kid's birthday, he's not going to appreciate having to convince a room full of crying first graders that baby carrots are a delicious substitute for chocolate cupcakes. Believing your child is the golden exception to every rule is how kids grow up to behave like Justin Bieber. Is that your goal?

Try to resist the phrase "my child wouldn't do that." If the teacher is saying it, chances are that your child would.

Don't assume your teacher only gave your kid one night to do an entire science project or book

report. Before you go barging in yelling, "How can you expect Deuce to stay up until four a.m. finishing this?" just know that the teacher most likely assigned the project weeks ago and sent home many flyers/e-mails since then that were never actually checked.

Understand that teachers are also people with home lives, and sometimes they even dare to have kids of their own. A teacher's life: super cush, right? Don't they just show up in the morning mere moments before the kids do to open the classroom and then jam out of there the second class is dismissed so they can spend the afternoon watching reruns of *Saved by the Bell*? Ha ha. No. But it's so funny that you thought that! Teachers actually work a lot of hours. And they bring their work home. I've heard of teachers who actually have to grade papers well into *The Bachelorette*. I mean, obviously if it's the night of the Final Rose no homework would have been assigned. But other than that, teachers are actually quite busy.

It's always a struggle to figure out the perfect end-of-year teacher gift. Do you go with a simple gift card? Just pitch in on the class gift? What about specialty gourmet ice cream flown in from an artisan ice creamery in Montana because you think you heard her mention she'd like to eat a pint of Ben & Jerry's that one time? I know. It's hard to decide. So rather than give you suggestions on what to get, I thought I'd help more by telling you what they probably won't enjoy.

1. A photo of your child blown up to poster size. Yes, his teacher likes him, but probably not that much. If she does, you actually may have gotten Mary Kay Letourneau. Seriously, look into it. She's out on parole.

2. An iTunes gift card for ten bucks. Nothing says "I really couldn't take thirty seconds to think about who you are and what you might actually like" more earnestly than an iTunes gift card.

3. You showing up in your nicest pajama pants for the last-day-of-school drop-off *and* pickup.

4. A card that says, "Yeah, thanks for doing your job."

5. A Nickelback CD.

6. Four booster credits for Candy Crush. I mean, four? Really? At least spring for six.

7. A half bottle of your kid's leftover Ritalin.

8. A gift certificate for a session of "classy boudoir photography."

9. Nits.

Just Like Jerry Springer, I've Got Some Final Thoughts

- - - -- -- -- -- --- -

Throughout this book I've shared my opinions, attitudes, and yes, I'm sure a few bits of advice even though *I really didn't mean to*! I meant to share my experiences only and let you draw your own conclusions, but sometimes advice just slipped out uninvited—like Lil' Kim's nipple—so you have my permission to go ahead and ignore anything I wrote that didn't resonate with you. You'd actually be following my advice anyway, because it's basically this: trust your instincts! You know what's best for your kids. Hell, you're the one who lives with them day after day after ever-long day. Why should you listen to Dr. Spock, Dr. Phil, or some A-list celeb who tells *Us Weekly* that you can cure your kid's psoriasis with pancake batter?

Most people don't know what the hell they're talking

about anyway. I once wrote an article about one of my twins who had failure to thrive. My little girl was a tiny peanut who barely ate, and my husband and I were incredibly worried and on a mission to get to the bottom of it. Our daughter was under the care of therapists, nutritionists, and a pediatric GI. But luckily for us, there were also people with no medical expertise in digestive issues whatsoever who were willing to give us some good, old-fashioned, commonsense straight talk! They e-mailed me: "Stop trying to feed her! Kids will eat when they're hungry!" Fantastic! Let me pass your findings on to the professionals; they'll be so relieved you're on the case!

So no, I'm not trying to tell you what to do. I'm just trying to help you feel a skosh less crazy. That's my goal. Because the truth is, you aren't crazy, even though parenting these days makes you feel like it. We put pressure on ourselves to live up to these monumental expectations of being the perfect parent: volunteering at their schools, reading to them every single day, making nutritious meals, teaching good values, keeping them off of electronics. Those, my friends, are lofty goals. The truth is, some days you are going to suck at parenting. Some days you are going to drop your kids in front of a *Zoey 101* marathon for six hours because you absolutely need to get some work done.

Other days they will be glued to their iPads and you simply won't be able to summon the strength to set some proper limits. Some nights they're going to eat Fruity Pebbles for dinner. And there will be times your four-year-old will hit a kid in the face with a Wiffle bat, and when they both come to you crying, you will make the wrong call and blame the other kid. Take those days in stride. Even pro baseball players can strike out a lot and still maintain a decent batting average.

But once in a while it will be worse. Much worse. Once in a while, you're going to seriously lose your shit. It could happen on the last day of summer vacation when it's *you* who needs a break from the unrelenting weeks of togetherness, or it could just be a random Tuesday after you worked all day and cooked a dinner that your kids made a face at and refused to eat. When you ask them to get into the bath they'll ignore you and go back to watching TV. You'll look around the house and notice that your kids have been eating granola bars and just tossed the wrappers on the floor! I mean, do they have that little respect? Why do they treat the house like a dump? Just the other day you bought them a Lego Friends beach house that cost $39.99 after they *promised* they would be better listeners and clean up after themselves. Who do they think is supposed to clean it up?

Are you their maid? And while you're walking around cleaning up after them, you won't be able to help but think that you're raising totally entitled spoiled brats! And by the way, you've asked them to get in the bath thirty times, but no one is listening to you and they won't stop *bickering* and suddenly you snap and scream, "*Just get in the fucking bath!*"

And then you freeze because, oh shit! Your personal parenting code of conduct doesn't allow for swearing around your kids, let alone *at* your kids! You've hit a new low! And they look at you, stunned and hurt for a moment, and then run off to the bath. For a second you feel justified and angry but mere moments later you sink into despair and wonder how you turned into such a horrible mom. A mom who would lose it like that on her kids!

Well, guess what. You swore. It's not the end of the world. You aren't a horrible parent. You yelled and you used a bad word. They've heard worse. They watch cable.

Here's what you need to do: you need to go into their room and you need to apologize. Explain to them that Mommy was having a bad day and got a little frustrated and said a bad word. You tell them that you are very sorry and that it's never okay to talk to them that way and then reassure them about how you love them. Remind them that you can't even imagine a time that they weren't on this planet. Let them know exactly how special they are and that they inspire you to do better. Apologizing to your kids is powerful stuff. And kids are incredibly forgiving. For reals. Now hug it out.

Try not to feel bad. You're doing better than your parents did. Hell yeah you are! Sure, there are things your parents did right—and you try to pass those things along to your kids—but there is plenty they did wrong, and you learned from their mistakes and are trying to improve upon them. You just need to put it in perspective: You aren't that pageant mom who allegedly gave her eight-year-old daughter Botox so she wouldn't get wrinkles! Feel better about your parenting now? Or what about the "Human Barbie" lady who gifted her seven-year-old with a voucher for a boob job that she can use when she turns sixteen? Or how about the drunky dad who made his eight-year-old drive on the freeway so he could sleep it off while his four-year-old was unbelted in the backseat? Look those people up, and then throw yourself a parade! Compared to these people, you are doing fantastic. Okay, at least you aren't newsworthy! And some days, you just gotta take "not newsworthy" as a win. At least that's my advice!